SCENES FROM THE PAST : 37 (PART (

RAILWAYS OF THE HIGH

WHALEY BRIDGE
TO
FRIDEN

Briggs Sidings, June 28th 1965. With the 13.40 Friden to Buxton working in tow, Ivatt Class 2 2-6-0 No **46401** (9L) moves out of the shadows of the Dowlow Lime complex. The train comprises a 'mixed bag' of wagons principally low sided with track sleepers (behind the engine) and steel mineral wagons containing limestone. Immediately against the brake van is one of the old tenders used for transporting water; it would be filled at Buxton depot and returned to the High Peak line. Notwithstanding the deviations of the Cromford & High Peak from it's early days - the dry stone wall to the left marks the original alignment - brought about by the Buxton & High Peak Junctions projects of the 1880's, the section of route here is to this day the only remaining operational piece of the erstwhile C&HP. Nowadays, this location serves as the truncated remains of a single line branch from Buxton. *E.F.Bentley*

NORMAN JONES & MICHAEL BENTLEY

Designed and Edited by Gregory K. Fox,
Norman Jones and Paul Shackcloth.
Typeset by Norman Jones and Paul Shackcloth
Printed by: Amadeus Press, Huddersfield

Published by Foxline Publishing
32 Urwick Road, Romiley, Stockport SK6 3JS

Newhaven Road Crossing, 2 April 1965: On arrival at the crossing, Fireman Dennis Valence proceeded to open the crossing gates which protected the Via Gelia road, the key for which was attached to the train-staff for the Longcliffe - Friden section. The long-since demolished crossing keeper's house can just be seen beyond locomotive No **68079**; note the wooden shutters attached to the cab side to give the footplate crew extra protection. *J.M.Bentley*

(Inset)
Hillhead Sidings. Closing Years: A view from the footplate of an Ivatt 2MT 2-6-0 propelling a lengthy train out of the sidings towards Harpur Hill. The brake van can be seen proceeding round the distant curve in the line. *J.M.Bentley*

Whaley Bridge c.1892: In 1854, supported by the L&NWR, the Stockport, Disley & Whaley Bridge Railway received its Act; the line was opened on 9th June 1857, and the official connection to the Cromford & High Peak Railway was opened on the 17th August following. This picture shows the main line station after extension following the removal of a level crossing adjacent to the signal box (left). The works are illustrated in the following pages, and beyond the standing figure are the original and lower platforms, the new ones being constructed to a higher level. **G. K. Fox collection**

INTRODUCTION

Several scholarly works have dealt with the history of the Cromford & High Peak Railway, but in this book the intention of your authors and their publisher is to present in the popular and explicit Foxline *SCENES FROM THE PAST* format a profusely illustrated account of the High Peak line as the working railway that we and the late respected railway historian Dr J. R. Hollick and his associates knew so well; to show something of its niche in rural life and something of its relationship with those railwaymen who served this unique railway over generations, enlivening the story with an account of some of the trials and tribulations that beset the hardy staff of a unique railway some of whose working practices dated back to the primitive horse-tramroads of the late 18th century.

The "30th Anniversary of Closure Events Programme" of the Cromford & High Peak Railway in 1997, and the recent publication of Foxline's book "Railways of the High-Peak *BUXTON TO ASHBOURNE*" (which has been so well received) seemed a good time to undertake a nostalgic trip to Derbyshire, where much of the route of the railway that I knew well in its working life is now preserved as the eighteen mile long High Peak Trail, stretching from High Peak Wharf on the Cromford Canal to just beyond Hurdlow Wharf on the Monyash to Longnor road.

This recreational track way is reserved for walkers, cyclists (cycles can be hired at the visitor centres) and horse-riders, and whilst access is easy, the best places to join the trail are the old stations (or wharfs, for the Cromford & High Peak Railway had a canal heritage) at Hurdlow, Parsley Hay, Friden, Minninglow, Middleton Top Engine House, Black Rocks and High Peak Junction, the latter on the Cromford Canal.

A visit to Middleton Top Engine House was high on the agenda, to view the preserved beam engine, which I last saw working in 1962, when preparing an article for *AD REM*, the house magazine of The Butterley Co., Ltd., who were celebrating 172 years of achievement in the heavy engineering industry, the text included by kind permission of J. Exon Esq., Managing Director of the company today.

THE LONG PULL - After 130 years, a Butterley-built engine still hauls wagons up Britain's steepest railway' by Norman Jones. "Amongst the many monuments to Butterley engineering skill which can be found all over the world, the condensing type engine at the Middle Top Winding House of Derbyshire's Cromford & High Peak Railway is by no means the most well known. Yet it deserves its own particular place in the history of the company's many years of achievement, because it is the last of eight which the Butterley Iron Works built for the railway between 1825 and 1829 and it is still working efficiently today. Middleton Top is a section of the Cromford & High Peak line - Britain's steepest railway- which is divided into two parts. The first section runs from Cromford to Parsley Hay where it joins the railway from Ashbourne to Buxton. The second leaves the Ashbourne/Buxton line beyond Hindlow and continues to Ladmanlow where it stops. The original idea behind these little-known stretches of railway was to link the Cromford Canal with the Peak Forest Canal at Whaley Bridge, but lack of water supplies to fill any new cut led to the scrapping of the scheme. Instead, the Cromford & High Peak Railway was authorised by Act of Parliament in 1825 and the 33 route miles were finally in full operation by 1831. Later developments were in connection with the Manchester, Buxton, Matlock & Midlands Junction Railway at High Peak Junction; and, at the Whaley Bridge end of the line, with the Stockport Disley & Whaley Bridge Railway.

The line was curtailed in 1892, and as explained now finishes at Ladmanlow. *"The Middleton Top Winding House was designed to assist trains to surmount the 708 yards incline to the Middleton Top itself, where the 1,000 feet contour line is encountered. This stretch of track has a 253 ft vertical rise and a gradient of 1 in 8°. Originally the route was single-line, but it was doubled in 1894. Chains were used when the railway opened but a change was made to hemp rope in 1855; this method lasted only for six years and wire rope was introduced in 1861.*

Wagons are attached to an endless rope of 1,760 yards length by a tapering chain ending in leather straps. They are balanced whenever possible i.e. descending wagons by ascending wagons and the winding engine is then used as a controlling medium only."
The Maximum speed is 8 mph and the permitted loading:

Balanced Up :	1 load or 3 empties
Balanced Down:	2 loads or 5 empties
Winding Up / Down	2 loads or 5 empties

The engine at Middleton Top itself is a massive piece of equipment. Built at the Butterley Iron Works in 1825, it is a 20 h.p condensing beam engine with two cylinders, having a 25in diameter and 60in stroke. The flywheel is 14ft in diameter and a Lancashire boiler operates at a pressure of 5 lbs per square inch. The engine is wood-fired with offcuts etc., which are transported regularly from the Carriage and Wagon Works at Derby.

Yet another link with the beginning of the unique Cromford line can be found in the grey stone cottage beside the Winding House. Here resides Tom Hallows, a member of the family which helped to build the railway, and when the job was done, worked as ostlers, for before locomotives were installed, horses used to pull wagons between the inclines. To our Georgian ancestors, the Middleton Top Winding engine must indeed have seemed a marvel of engineering skill and even today its huge cylinders and great flywheel command respect. Nowadays the line is used solely for commercial work following a fatal accident to a passenger many years ago."

Whaley Bridge. L&NWR main line. c.1890: The Cromford & High Peak Railway passed beneath the Manchester to Buxton line at this point and at the bottom of the edge of the picture, extending to the right-hand corner, is a connecting line to the Whaley Bridge Incline, on which stand at least two five-plank wagons. Across the line is the 'Old Shaft' the building in part housing and in part structure of an 18th century beam engine. Subsidence from the old Shallcross Colliery workings were a constant problem. ***J.M.Bentley collection***

Whaley Bridge. L&NWR c.1890: On a day of 'typical north Derbyshire weather' with the area around Bridge No 38 shrouded in mist, two-wheeled horse-drawn tip-carts of the period are being used by labourers engaged in work in connection with the removal of the level crossing at the station referred to in our introduction. In view of the slow film emulsions of the period, although this was a 'posed' scene, the light - such as it was - would hardly have allowed for early morning photography so perhaps the neatly dressed schoolboys are on their 'dinner break.' Beyond the main line a plethora of small mills and collieries and rows of terraced houses add their quota of smoke to the already laden atmosphere. *J.M.Bentley Collection*

Now, over two hundred years since the company was first established, Butterley Engineering Ltd, of Ripley, Derbyshire, trade through three divisions of Bridges & Structures, Cranes & Machines and Materials Handling, designing and manufacturing specialist engineering products for major industries worldwide, using the most up to date disciplines the company policy being that; *"the qualities of craftsmanship, innovation, quality and dependability are as important today as when our forefathers were laying the foundations of the first Industrial Revolution."*

In the Acknowledgements to *SCENES FROM THE PAST : No 32 RAILWAYS OF THE HIGH PEAK BUXTON to ASHBOURNE* authors Michael Bentley and Gregory K. Fox write with affection of the legendary Dr J. R. Hollick, and this work is intended to complement the Foxline series of High Peak books inspired by Doctor Hollick's absorbing interest in the area and its railway, particularly since before his death, Dr Hollick presented Mike Bentley with his unique "High Peak Notebook" containing detailed hand-written accounts and meticulously drawn maps of the Doctor's observations and researches into the Cromford & High Peak Railway over four decades commencing in 1932. The note book's contents are the framework on which this generously illustrated tribute is based.

Joanna Neal has compiled this obituary to her late father, Dr J. R. Hollick (Charterhouse, 1928) who died on 26th September 1991 :

"John Reginald Hollick was born in 1910 in Ashbourne, Derbyshire, the only son of a much loved general practitioner. After going down from Oxford he completed his training as a doctor at the London Hospital. There is a suggestion that he might have preferred to remain in London and become a surgeon. However, he joined his father in general practice in Ashbourne in 1938 where he remained until his retirement in 1972. He married his wife Barbara in 1943 and they had five children.

Outside medical matters, John Hollick had an interest in railway history. He was co-author of *The North Staffordshire Railway (1949)* and *The Leek and Manifold Light Railway (1955).* He was also the author of many articles in railway magazines. His collection of photographs has been widely used by other railway authors to illustrate their books. In 1973 he became editor of the Historical Model Railway Society journal, carrying out this role for many years. [A near-contemporary and railway enthusiast, A. J. F. Wrottesley (1926) quotes .... his wide knowledge of the railways in Staffordshire, which was unsurpassed, and his anecdotes made him a popular speaker. He was always willing to share his knowledge with fellow enthusiasts'.] His other major interest was philately. Dr Hollick, who retired in 1972 to Hartington in the Peak District, suffered a severe stroke in 1990."

The C&HPR that Dr Hollick and your authors knew in its working days, (myself as a free-lance technical author and industrial photographer producing material for British Rail's, London Midland Region Magazine amongst other assignments, and colleague Michael Bentley as BR footplate man at Buxton) was very much the same Cromford & High Peak Railway which had operated under London & North Western Railway management, following their leasing of the line for a term of 999 years on 25th March 1861.

Two decades later there were about 50 trains per day on the High Peak Railway, of which the fastest (through train) took just over five hours (including working up/down the inclines, changing the engines and shunting as required) to cover the 32.5 miles, separating the Cromford Canal, and Midland Railway at Whatstandwell, from the Peak Forest Canal and London & North Western Railway system at Whaley Bridge. When the L&NW and Midland Railways opened, their lines into Buxton in 1863, the C&HPR could no longer claim to provide a viable 'through route' for passengers and a passenger coach may have been superseded by the addition of 'break' vans to specified trains; the majority of the passengers were Buxton Lime Co., employees on their way to/from work; the Hoffman Kiln at Harpur Hill with its 80 foot high chimney, that was to dominate the countryside until dismantled in 1952, was built in 1872 whilst in 1881 the Buxton Lime Co's works, said to be the largest in the country, was served by 12 miles of internal railways and tramways.

On our recent visit to the High Peak we visited the Tourist and Information centres with their friendly staff, but engineer Tony Robinson and I had difficulty in equating the pleasant bridle-paths with the busy railways of the 1950's. The restoration of the Butterley engine at Middleton Top is 'brilliant' but as it was driven by compressed air, we missed the smell of hot oil, the hiss of minor steam leaks and occasional splash of condensate from the glands, and the awesome impression of power when the engine was actually winding, and the subterranean rumble as the wire rope passed over the drum. A stroll down the incline, passing the single wooden bodied ex Midland Wagon marooned on a short length of track at the top, even the presence of a semaphore signal did little to recreate one's mental image of the former broad expanse of double track, the singing of the pulleys and busy clatter of the cable as a rake of wagons descended to Middleton Bottom, perhaps balanced by the ascent of an ancient converted McConnell tender transporting water to supply the reservoir at Middleton Top, scenes we hope to re-create in these books.

Whaley Bridge. L&NWR. c.1890. Nearby stood the JODRELL ARMS HOTEL. John William Jodrell, landowner of Yeardsley Hall, Taxal, for whom the inn was named, sold to Manchester business man Samuel Grimshawe II, 2,056 acres of his Taxal valley, where Grimshawe built the Italianate Errwood Hall and estate cottages and farms, in the valley later flooded when acquired by the Stockport Corporation as a site for their Fernilee and Errwood reservoirs.

J.M.Bentley collection

Whaley Bridge. L&NWR. c.1890: This work was carried out adjacent to Bridge No 38, illustrated on Page 5, and the proximity of the station is evident in this picture, for the station buildings are observed to the left of the two boys peering down from the wall in the top right-hand corner of the scene as is a corner of the lattice girder foot-bridge which spanned the platforms shown in our opening view of the station. The imposing looking gentleman with the high collar and mutton-chop whiskers holding a pose in the foreground is obviously a person of some authority. *J.M.Bentley Collection*

HISTORY

The Cromford & High Peak Railway was projected as a canal to link up the Cromford Canal (authorised 1789) and the Whaley Bridge branch of the Peak Forest Canal (opened 1800). It was then realised that insufficient water would be obtainable on the limestone heights and the plan was modified to cover the construction of a railway. But the pattern of canal engineering was retained and the line was built with nine long gradients of varying severity (equivalent to flights of locks) and sections between them which were practically level; these would have been 'pounds' had the canal been built.

The railway was authorised by *Act 6 Geo. IV. Cap. 30 of 2 May 1825* and seven years were allowed for the construction.

The line was opened on 29 May 1830 from Cromford Wharf to Hurdlow (15.5 miles) and forward to Whaley Bridge (a further 17 miles) in July 1831.

The Cromford & High Peak Railway was re-incorporated by *Act 18 and 19 Vic. Cap. 75 of 26 June 1855,* and this Act included authority for carrying passengers.

The C&HP was leased to the L&NWR with effect from 25th March 1861 although this was not authorised until 30 June 1862. The line was finally vested in the L&NWR by Act of 19 July 1887.

The L&NWR was authorised by *Act of 4 August 1890,* to abandon the C&HP north of Ladmanlow (except for a short length at Whaley Bridge) and to construct a new line from Buxton to Hurdlow; to realign the C&HP between Ladmanlow and Parsley Hay as necessary, to eliminate the sharpest curves and to construct a new line from Parsley Hay to Ashbourne.

Left: Whaley Bridge, May 1998. Right: The same spot c.1930's. Amongst the major 'artifacts' demanding attention when visiting the area is an inspection of the still extant High Peak Railway's handsome wrought-iron girder bridge at the foot of the former Whaley Bridge Incline that, together with the Wharf was closed on the 10th April 1952. The 189 yard long incline with a gradient of 1 in 13 which terminated in a basin of the Peak Forest Canal was worked by horsepower when it first opened to traffic, e.g. a horse circled round and round a horizontal 'gin' that rotated a capstan to drive the endless winding cable to which the wagons were attached. During this early period a two cylinder 10 hp steam powered winding engine was installed, but proved unsatisfactory due to mining subsidence disturbing the land beneath the incline, and by 1862 equine motive power was again in use and no further attempts were made to use a stationary engine. As will be observed by the subject of the second picture, accidents could happen!

G.K.Fox & J.M.Bentley Collection

These projects were completed as under:

Hindlow to Ladmanlow - realignment 27 June 1892

Buxton to Hindlow - new line 27 June 1892

Ladmanlow to Shallcross abandoned 25 June 1892 and line taken up in sections during 1892 - 1894

Hindlow to Parsley Hay - realignment and doubling 1st June 1894

Parsley Hay to Ashbourne - new line - 4 August 1899

Five inclines raised the line from Cromford (278 ft above sea level) to the summit level just north of Hurdlow and extending to north of Ladmanlow. The height was originally stated as 1254 feet but later expressed as 1266 feet. Four inclines took the line down to 517 feet above sea level at Whaley Bridge.

Stationary engines by the Butterley Co., Ltd., hauled the wagons up the inclines and horses worked the traffic on the level sections, until the first locomotive was introduced soon after 1840.

From 1856 to 1877 passengers were conveyed by one daily goods train throughout the length of the line. A guard's van including a passenger compartment and known as the 'fly' was run for them. Passengers had to walk up and down the inclines. The journey time throughout for the 33 miles was from 5 to 6 hours depending upon circumstances.

Until the opening of the Midland branch from Millers Dale to Buxton on 1st June 1863 **and the line from Whaley Bridge to Buxton** on 15 June 1864, the C&HP provided the only rail access to the vicinity of Buxton, passengers using **"Parkes Platform"**, Harpur Hill.

The Cromford & High Peak Railway played a vital role during the years of World War II and remained so after nationalisation but it was subject to the pressures financial and political that led to the emasculation of our railway system and closure dates of sections and services of the C&HPR during the period of British Railways control were on the northern section:

Whaley Bridge Incline and Wharf - 10 April 1952

Old Harpur to Ladmanlow - 2 August 1954

Passenger services withdrawn, Buxton to Parsley Hay, Ashbourne - 1st November 1954

Line singled: Parsley Hay to Briggs Siding - 21 June 1959

Friden reclassified as a coal depot - 6 July 1964

Shallcross Yard to Whaley Bridge station - 30 January 1965

Old Harpur to Harpur Hill - 2 February 1966

Friden to Parsley Hay - 2 October 1967

Parsley Hay to Briggs Siding - 2 November 1967

Harpur Hill to Hindlow - 19 September 1973

Canal Warehouses & Transhipment Sheds at Whaley Bridge around the turn of the last century: Marple industrialist Samuel Oldknow was a major promoter of the Peak Forest Canal that runs 14 miles from its commencement at the Ashton Canal, Dukinfield to Whaley Bridge Junction, where it forks into a half-mile junction to the Sheds and Wharves at Whaley Bridge, and a three-quarter mile branch to Bugsworth Basin. Engineered by Benjamin Outram, together with William Jessop two separate levels of the canal were opened by 1801, connected by a tramway for some four years, whilst the Marple flight of 16 locks was completed. Reservoirs at Toddbrook and Coombes supplied the canal with water and an inlet from the latter was inside one of the sheds.

J.M.Bentley collection

Whaley Bridge

Whaley Bridge c.1998: If today's visitors having traversed the attractive linear park into which the local council have converted the former trackbed of the Cromford & High Peak Railway, continue over the historic bowstring girder bridge depicted on the previous page, they will observe adjacent to this Car Park the terminus of the Peak Forest Canal and the splendid and quite imposing warehouses, seemingly in as sound condition as when built in 1832. *G.K.Fox*

CONNECTIONS WITH OTHER RAILWAYS

CONNECTIONS WITH OTHER RAILWAYS were opened as follows: Junction with the Manchester, Buxton, Matlock & Midlands Junction Railway (1 mile from Cromford Wharf to High Peak Junction) was opened on 21 February 1853. The MBM&MJR had been opened from Ambergate to Rowsley on 4 June 1849, and was leased to the Midland and London & North Western Railways jointly from 1 July 1852. It acquired the Cromford Canal on 30 August 1852. A junction with the

Stockport, Disley & Whaley Bridge Rly (1/4 mile) was opened on 17 August 1857. The SD&WBR was opened on 9 June 1857, and was extended to Buxton on 15 June 1864, and acquired by the L&NWR in 1866.

In the course of his researches Dr J. R. Hollick accumulated a wealth of anecdotal material from the early days of the C&HPR and we are indebted to his researches for the following:

SIMILARITIES BETWEEN CANAL AND RAILWAY WORKING

From the outset the C&HPR with its inclines replacing flights of locks, and the level stretches between them equating to the upper 'pounds' of the waterways suffered from its 'Canal' heritage, The similarity was heightened by the traffic being handled by private Carriers, who used either their own trucks, or wagons hired from the railway company, also supplying their own horses. The working methods followed canal practice, 'stations' were designated 'Wharfs' and the men who worked at them 'Wharfingers'.

The Derby Mercury carried a report in 1833 that 'Wheatcrofts' - a firm with waterway expertise- had taken out a licence to carry passengers on the C&HPR. In the narrative entitled "Recollections of Seventy Years Ago" which follows, Mr C. Woodhouse (born 20 March 1857) tells of his father's four decades of service on the C&HPR as flyman in the period when horses were employed. One horse could draw a load of ten tons on rails as opposed to one ton on a good road; it appears that during this period, passengers stayed on the fly-coach during its traverse of the inclines a practice which would appal today's Health & Safety Executive officials but which the travellers probably preferred to the arduous and equally dangerous alternative of walking up and down the inclines.

The Whaley Incline

The Whaley Bridge Incline c.1952: When this picture was taken the fate of the incline was already decided and although a wagon stands at the foot of the ascent, the winding cables have been removed, and the guide pulleys stand idle, although a cast-iron L&NWR warning notice is still in position on the left-hand side. The presence of the rows of terraced houses and the mill chimneys emphasise the fact that the 180 yard long Whaley Bridge incline and of course the C&HPR ended almost in the town centre. *E.M.Johnson collection*

Having ascended the Whaley Bridge incline this paved section of double track was encountered, the remains of the horse-operated capstan which operated the winding cables can be distinguished on the bend in the distance. *G.K.Fox collection*

The chain-horse seems to be doing most of the work in this picture of traditional working at the top of the Whaley Bridge incline not long before its closure. *G.K.Fox collection*

A FAMILY AFFAIR
Mr. C. Woodhouse

'I must state that I am the last survivor of three generations of employees of the old Cromford and High Peak Railway. My grandfather helped to build the line from the top of Middleton incline to Hopton; my father had 39 years service on the line as flyman, and I myself, born 20 March 1857, was on the line in the old offices at Cromford Station.

My father was first employed as flyman before steam was introduced, when the line was worked by horsepower. The flyman's van was an old goods van, with a passenger compartment at one end. The remainder of the space was left for goods traffic, which the flyman had to deliver along the line.

I should say that passenger traffic continued for many years until it was brought to an end by a head-on accident between the through train leaving Ladmanlow and a lime train leaving for Harpur Hill meeting on 17 December 1875.

When the line was run by horses (both fly and slow) the men used to work by marks at certain distances apart. I have heard my father describe how they used to run to a mark. If they did not reach it in time they turned back to let the other train pass. I have heard him say that all the stone for the front of St George's Hall, Liverpool was taken over the line from Darley Dale. The material was carted from there to Cromford and loaded at the wharf just past the Post Office at High Peak Junction. The five cottages below belonged to J. Arkwright, but were leased to the C&H Peak Railway for workmen. I was born in the middle house and all my earliest recollections are of that district.

At that time the wharf at **Cromford** was in divisions. There was a warehouse, at which a boat was kept for use in taking goods to Lea, Lea Mills and Holloway. From the first to the second bend of the canal the wharf was utilised by the Hopton Wood Stone Company whose stone was sent from their works in four ton waggons and stacked on the wharf for loading into boats.

The next wharf was let to the Butterley Company, who had the Intake Quarry between Middleton and Hopton inclines. Across the road for Brown's Bridge over the canal , there was room for two boats to unload. On the sidings there was a workshop where a joiner and a wheelwright were employed. They were Mr Hawley and Mr Bagshaw respectively. Chain-maker (William Robins), Tom Sheldon (Blacksmith), Edward Farmer (Mechanic), Samuel Bullivant and his father Thomas Bullivant were in the other workshop. Thomas Bullivant was engineer of the line, followed by Edward Farmer. James Reed was in the old weighing machine office. At one time Sheep-pasture was in two portions, also Bonsall plane, and for connection they were worked with chain prior to wire ropes.

(Right) c.1960: "To boldly go!" Rebuilt 'Scot' No **46152** *The King's Dragoon Guardsman* from 6J (Holyhead) carries a Class J headlamp (mineral or empty wagon train) having negotiated the loading gauge (above) slips stealthily beneath the A625 road bridge beside the platelayer's cabin to make an unexpected and startling appearance in Shallcross Yard.
J.M.Bentley

The lines around Whaley Bridge: The Wharf and Incline at Whaley Bridge were closed in April 1952, although Shallcross Yard continued to handle traffic. Lines running between rows of terraced houses were 'of their time' and the former L&NWR antecedents of the route to Whaley and to the Wharf (see maps) are emphasised by the typical cast-iron notice, point lever, tall sleeper fence and signals
E.M.Johnson

On the route to Shallcross this loading gauge protected the arch of the road bridge that carried the A625 road across the railway, the camera lens was pointed in the direction of Whaley Bridge.
L.Hobdey

Whaley Bridge (Shallcross) LNWR: Whaley Bridge Goods was closed from 30 Jan 1965 but remained a "part unstaffed station/halt" until 2 August 1971. This view from the A625 road bridge depicts a busy scene with high-sided coke wagons for the gas works (right) whilst the ascending line of trees beyond the standing vehicles denote the route of the abandoned Shallcross Incline. It was at this point that No **46152** was seen on Page 11.   *E.M.Johnson*

Similarities between canal and railway working - continued

BOATMEN'S CABINS

Opposite F. Barton's coal wharf, where the present weighing machine stands, there used to be two or three cabins that housed the boatmen and plate layers, old James Austin and his brother Ned. Ned looked after Barton's coal and used to go with the boats to the coal-pit. Patrick Gafney worked for the HWS Company unloading stone. The warehouse staff in offices consisted of William Crofts and William Roper; Mr Leonard Hughes was stationmaster; Andrew Swift, John Weston, Peter Britland, George Ward and James Hardy carters. William Hardy and George Gardom were shunters to the junction. Everything had to be transhipped after coming up to the junction to our own trucks as the MR would not allow their waggons to go up the inclines. This kept all busy at the railway end, and I was in the office when the first trucks of Burton grains came in.

James Evans was the engine driver at the top of Sheep-pasture and there were two hangers on. Samuel Buxton was stationmaster for Sheep-pasture (written as Sheep pasture NJ). One or two horses were kept for delivery of goods in Wirksworth, Bolehill and Middleton. Guy Hall was the lorry-man. We went forward from here and, at the first bend there was the Butterley

Company's quarry (Intake); then there was **Hopton Tunnel** and the Hopton Wood Stone Company's Hopton quarry (HWS. NJ) The waggons were drawn up at that time by a stationary engine built between the railway and the Wirksworth road; Butler was the driver's name. The next stop was Thomas Taylor's bone mill and patent fertilisers, and then **Hopton Incline**, which was worked by endless chains. A man at the bottom, I believe a platelayer, hung the trucks on. Samuel Hallowes was the last stationary engine driver here, and he also had to hang the trucks on.

When the Parsley Hay and Ashbourne line was made, the contractor pulled this old engine house down and sent all the stonework to Levenshulme. It was said he was going to use the stone for building purposes. From **Hopton Top** we went forward to Messrs. Armytage's new saw mill. Blocks of stone were carted from Wetton Quarry and pink marble from the Duke of Devonshire's Wetton Hill Quarry. The next stop used to be **Longcliffe Station,** where Daniel Holmes was stationmaster. There was a lot of traffic here especially coal (F. BARTON); Mr Gould used to sell for him. We went along the line then until **Bloor's Siding** was reached; he first opened out the silica sand works at Minninglow. He had previously had works at Low Moor against the farm house and carted it to Minninglow Siding for Parwick and district under Longcliffe Station control.

Shallcross Sidings, Whaley Bridge nd:
No doubt the two pictures shown here were taken on the same date; the problem is just what date was it? Looking firstly at the DX goods 0-6-0 No **1590** most, if not all of those engines numbered between 1500 and 1599 were allocated to Longsight and Ordsall Lane depots, Manchester who farmed-out to the depots under their control the number of locomotives required by those depots to cover their work. No **1590** built in July 1867, could have been at Stockport Edgeley, or more possibly Buxton. It is seen here with its 'Webb' modifications carried out in the 1880's of cab and plain chimney top, but still no brakes on the loco, nor coal rails on the tender, indicating that the photograph was taken before 1895. The locomotive was broken up in September 1898 after being renumbered 3426 in the duplicate list of June that same year.

J.M.Bentley collection

Shallcross Sidings, Whaley Bridge nd: More clues as to date show themselves in this lower picture where staff are posing especially for the camera-man who, having in mind the slow film emulsions - the era of the wet collodion plate had not long passed - would have admonished them to "keep quite still" whilst he made the exposure. The incline cable is seen and appears to be in use, so this dates the period as being prior to 26 June 1892 when the Shallcross Incline was abandoned, along with that at Bunsal. The staff will include the men who tied on the wagons to the cable officially called 'hangers on', one holds a wooden sprag for jamming wagon wheels to obtain a braking effect by causing them to 'lock and skid', a wagon tapper with his hammer, a weigh-bridge man, shunters, per-way men and horse to draw wagons from Shallcross to the top of Whaley Incline; so - dare we say circa 1890 for these two pictures, what a pity that those unknown photographers did not take more views on the same day - or perhaps they did and they have been lost over the years!

J.M.Bentley collection

Proceeding further, we soon came to the celebrated **Gotham curve**, which frightened some drivers. The ganger always kept a supply of rails ready to replace broken ones as, if a driver took the curve too quickly, he split the rail. Next, one came to the **Newhaven** level crossing, managed by the wife of the foreman platelayer, the late Wm. Warrington and on to Friden. Proceeding, **Parsley Hay** was reached.

In the old days there was a long siding where the present station stands. Proceeding further along the line we came to **Hurdlow,** where there used to be an incline, but it was dispensed with and the present line was made by Messrs. Farnsworth, of Cromford and Matlock, which would be late in the sixties, or early seventies. A good length, it cut a long piece off the old line. Next came the old **Hindlow** station where Thomas Handley was agent. **Harpur Hill** and **Ladmanlow** were the next places.

The next section reached was the part that is now closed for the new line through Buxton, but the old line went forward to Bunsall Tunnel and along the **Bunsall** Incline where Mr Henry Roper was engineer, and had two men as hangers on. The line took a sharp bend by the side of the River Roach, which runs into the Mersey at Stockport. The old powder mill at **Fernilea** was next reached, followed by **Shawcross** Incline, (Shallcross) where Mr Dranfield was engineer, with two hangers on and two at the bottom. Shawcross Sidings (Shallcross) at the foot of the incline used to be a very busy place, trains of lime being sent into Lancashire and Yorkshire. Going forward the fly was taken in charge by George Jackson who did shunting here with a horse, and he took us forward to **Whaley Bridge** goods shed. William Handforth was the goods porter and Mr William Moorcroft the stationmaster. The old canal end was not in use only for works. The line was often snowed up in winter and those in charge of trains had to leave it and get home the best way they could.

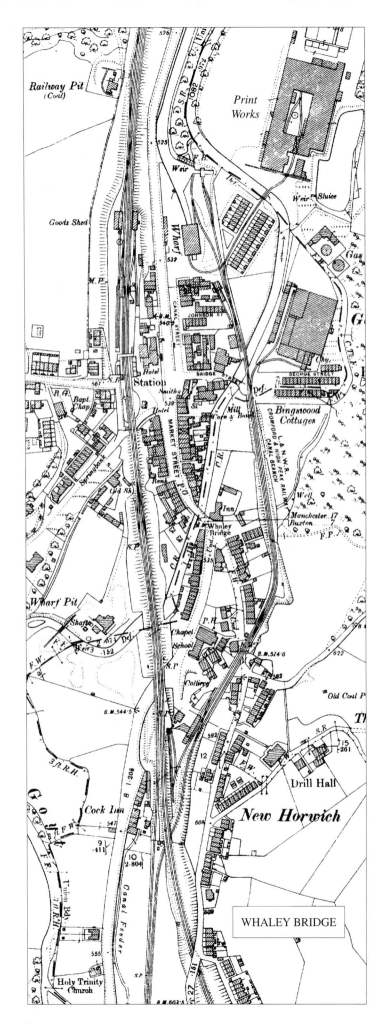

WHALEY BRIDGE

South from Shallcross

A public footpath between Elnor Road and Long Hill (A5004) affords this view of the abandoned section of the C&HP between the top of Shallcross Incline and Fernilee village. This view north shows the cluster of trees which marked the site of the engine house and locomotive shed. The gate posts on the left suggest a turnout or siding arrangement.

From the same viewpoint but looking south the disused trackbed continues towards Fernilee village, some of the buildings of which appear to the middle right of the picture. There is no public right of way along these parts of the erstwhile railway.

Minor realignment of Long Hill to the south of Fernilee village resulted in the filling in of the opening beneath the bridge C&HP No 61 carrying the Whaley Bridge to Buxton road (A5004). The parapet of the bridge can be seen in the foreground. The millstone signifies the boundary of the Peak District National Park. Compare this with the view below before infilling took place.   *Photographs G.K.Fox*

Into the Goyt Valley

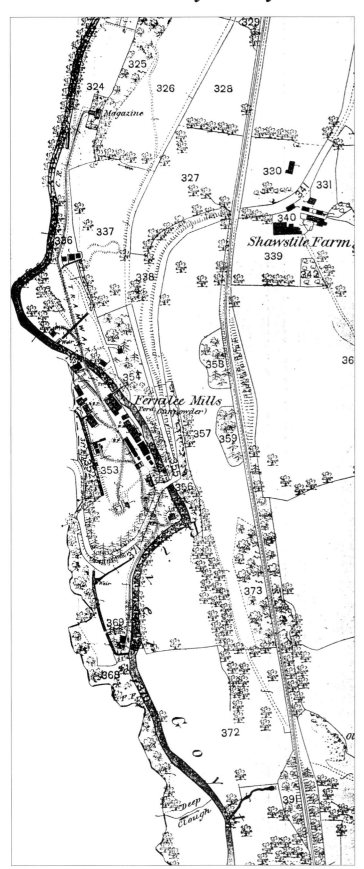

Occupants of road vehicles ascending Long Hill will catch a glimpse of the parallel stone walls that border the former railway. This section of line ran on the level from Shallcross Top right through to the bottom end of Bunsall Incline. There is, however, the sense of an optical illusion giving the impression that the railway was on a gradient.

The water company access road from Long Hill crosses the former C&HP trackbed nearby the reservoir dam. This is the view looking north towards Whaley Bridge.

In the opposite direction looking towards Bunsall, the alignment becomes part of the Fernilee Bridleway Concession, a facility extended by the Water Company for the public to enjoy the countryside. The waters of the reservoir at this point cover the site of the erstwhile Gunpowder Works.

(Right) Shallow cutting immediately to the south of the site of Shawstile Farm, (see map above) briefly screened the railway from the Gunpowder Works. This view south is towards Bunsall and vaitimately Cromford.

All photos: G.Fox

THE GOYT VALLEY RESERVOIRS

For almost forty years, this part of the track-bed once occupied by the lines of the Cromford & High Peak railway which had run along the side of the eastern slope of the Goyt Valley, would no longer resound to the sound of steam locomotives hard at work, and the area became a Mecca for walkers and 'hikers' in the late 1920's. These groups, amongst many members of the general public, were incensed by plans to 'flood' the valley, but, nevertheless after following the statutory procedures, the Stockport Corporation secured an Act of 1930 authorising construction of :

Work No 1 ERRWOOD RESERVOIR
Errwood reservoir, having a dam across the River Goyt 158 yards south-west of Bunsall farm.

Work No 2 FERNILEE RESERVOIR
Fernilee reservoir, with a dam carrying a public road across the River Goyt 413 yds north west of Shawstile farm.

In the late 1920's, early 1930's, public works on a massive scale were an important factor alleviating unemployment, so despite the depression, following the General Strike of 1926, which reduced industrial demand for water, the Stockport Corporation's area of influence, and population was increasing and planning to meet the demand for water, led to the Act of 1930, although construction of the Errwood reservoir was delayed until the 1960's. A grant towards the cost was obtained from the government's Unemployment Grants Committee, but the requirement that 90% of the workforce should be local was waived. A further Act of 1934 allowed modification of the original plans, involving an earth dam, its top 805 ft above Ordnance datum, and a top water level of 800 ft OD, with a capacity of 1,100 million gallons. The Errwood reservoir was inaugurated for the, then, Stockport & District Water Board by the Duchess of Kent on Friday, 14 June 1968.

Work on the Fernilee project commenced on Friday, 25 February 1932, the consulting engineers were Messrs G. H. Hill & Sons of Manchester, Mr H. P. Hill was the designing architect. Of eight tenders the main contract went, in Sept 1931, to Lehane, Mackenzie & Shand Ltd., of Derby, whose figure was £336,376 (excluding the shillings and pence!) The Corporation's Water Engineer was Mr Thomas Dearden and the site engineer for the contractors Mr W. J. Dyer.

During 1932-3, a 12 inch diameter, cast-iron high pressure pipeline was laid, using the cut and cover method along the old C&HPR track-bed beside the site of the proposed Fernilee reservoir, to take water from intakes and a small reservoir at Goyt's head to Higher Disley. A temporary 2 ft gauge railway was laid on the old formation, and 2 ft gauge lines were also laid during 'soil stripping'. At a quarry opened up at Upper Hall farm were two small steam locomotives, a Bagnall 0-4-0ST named simply 'B' and a 'Wren' class Kerr Stuart 0-4-0ST 'No 2'.

There was a 3ft gauge permanent railway, at Fernilee, and a self-acting incline from the new Issue Tor quarry, 1,000 ft up on the western slopes of the valley, and two stone-crushers to produce concrete making material. To excavate the foundation trench for the dam embankment, access gantries were built on the upstream side, with 3 ft gauge spurs on each, to carry the locomotive hauled construction trains, this phase was completed by Christmas 1933. The bank was then formed on both sides by trains of tip wagons bringing 'fill' from the valley bottom, and puddle-clay, from a puddle-field, downstream of the dam site, on the eastern side. Water was admitted into the reservoir from late September 1935. The works were declared to be open on Thursday, 10 June 1937, in time to meet the increased demand from Stockport's heavy industries as the country commenced to re-arm itself to face the threat of World War II.

THE 3FT GAUGE RESERVOIR RAILWAYS

The locomotive shed and site offices were on the eastern side of the valley, on a small plateau, adjoining the old Cromford & High Peak line, and the approach road; from this point the top of the dam and its downstream face were visible. About sixteen 3 ft gauge locomotives were seen at 'Fernilee' although not all at the same time; several had been used by Lehane's on other waterworks projects at Brownhill, Gorple, or occupied with other public works jobs. The oldest was *Heswall* an 0-4-0 ST o.c. 9 x 15 in Hudswell Clarke No **504** of 1898, amongst a range of vintages between '98 and 1925; Hudswell Clarke engines were well represented, as were Manning Wardle's and, W. G. Bagnall's, whilst of more exotic origin were an Orenstein and Koppell No **10903** of 1925 and *Darley Dale,* which was an 0-4-0 Well tank by Ducroo & Brauns No **42** also of 1925.

Special North Western Road Car Co Ltd buses brought workers from Stockport every day, but tradesmen and railway staff, e.g. workshop, loco men and permanent way staff, shunters, known as 'the black gang' lived in a small village of huts at the side of the approach road. In the summer of 1932 this group, with their families, included 107 adults and 25 children. 'Paddy trains' for the 'navvies' were not a feature of the contractor's railway, but

a saloon coach carrying a Kerr Stuart works plate that could be used as an inspection vehicle for council or other important officials, was included amongst the stock of tipping and other wagons.

An amusing sidelight of the original negotiations was that the L&MSR were unable to find the title deeds for the 1831 Cromford & High Peak line amongst their records, so rights to the land were transferred to the Stockport Corporation under a 'squatters' title. The old by-road bridge across the River Goyt was flooded, as was the old gunpowder mills, and the old house upstream of Fernilee dam; Errwood Hall was also demolished. A striking new feature was the handsome, white painted suspension bridge above the head of the new reservoir, built by Joseph Parkes & Son, which was removed when work on the Errwood reservoir, also by contractors Lehane, Mackenzie & Shand, began in the 1960's. But, the scars of building have now been obscured by the passage of years, up the once fearsome Bunsall Incline of the former C&HPR cars now drive to the upper part of the valley, to the average visitor, the reservoirs are attractive 'water features' whilst mountain bikers now share with walkers, the public path that is the route of the former Cromford & High Peak Railway.

Goyt Valley/Gunpowder Mills/Magazine.
c.1932: Two years following the sale of the splendid contents of Errwood Hall, over five days from 16 to 20 June, 1930 by Macclesfield auctioneers Turner & Son on the instructions of Miss E. E. H. Preston and Miss A. E. M. Preston, the peace and quiet of the Goyt Valley was shattered as the construction of the Fernilee Reservoir went ahead, contractors Lehane Mackenzie & Shand bringing in the latest mechanical equipment to assist in the task, although this was still an age when small industrial locomotives running on narrow gauge tracks were the norm on sites of this nature. There had been a ford across the River Goyt, adjacent to the Fernilee (Gunpowder) Mills which went out of production in 1920. The ruins, situated towards the dam wall end can sometimes be seen when water levels are low. *Mrs.E.Barton collection*

Goyt Valley/GunpowderMills/Demolition:
Around 1800, industrialist Thomas Williamson purchased the site for his enterprise from Francis Jodrell Esq; as with all such mills an isolated spot was chosen to carry on this dangerous trade, the products being supplied to mines and quarries in the area. For obvious safety requirements the magazine was situated some distance away from the factory, to which it was linked by narrow gauge tramways. Minor accidents were not uncommon, but the worst occurred in 1909 resulting in the death of three workers. Many such mills were abandoned as the nineteenth century progressed. There was a dreadful explosion at such a mill on the Mersey & Irwell Navigation at Thelwall, and the scattered ruins still mark the spot near the old Weir at Woolston, here they lie beneath the waters of Fernilee Reservoir.

Mrs.E.Barton collection

To carry water from intakes and a small reservoir at Goyt's Head to Higher Disley, a 12 in diameter cast-iron pipe was laid by 'cut and cover' methods along the old route of the C&HPR; to expedite the work a temporary 2ft gauge track was laid and contractors Lehane, Mackenzie and Shand imported two small steam engines to work on the line. No 2 pictured here was a 'Wren' class loco, Works No **3114** of 1918 delivered new in that year to the Ministry of Munitions at Driffield. She makes a charming picture simmering in the sunshine whilst her crew pose for their photograph on the former route of the Cromford & High Peak Railway at Fernilee in the Goyt Valley. *Mrs.E.Barton collection*

3 Foot Gauge Locomotives observed at Fernilee in the 1930's at work for contractors Lehane, Mackenzie & Shand Ltd., of Derby.

Taff Fawr was a product of the well known firm of W.G.Bagnall, an 0-4-0 Saddle Tank with outside cylinders 10 in x 16 in, she was younger than her companions on this page, having been built in 1923, with the Works No **2219**. Perhaps because of her 'youth' she is understood to have still been at Fernilee at the end of 1937, before appearing at Darley Dale two years later. During the years of World War II *Taff Fawr* was engaged on War Work in Scotland but was scrapped in the early 1950's. **J.Peden collection**

Water Works Saddle Tanks

Fernilee. 11 Aug 1934: *Derby* was an 0-4-0 Saddle tank with outside cylinders 9 in x 13 in, built by Manning Wardle & Co., Ltd., Boyne Engine Works, Hunslett, Leeds, Works No **1603** of 1904. No 1603 was removed from the contract by 1937 and sold on some five years later, going to the Admiralty in Scotland and subsequently putting in an appearance at Swansea around 1945. *Derby* was broken up for scrap c.1951.

B.D.Stoyel - J.Peden collection

Fernilee. c.1933: *Brownhill,* another 0-4-0 Saddle tank, but with slightly larger outside cylinders 9.5 in x 14 in was a product of the Hunslet Engine Co Ltd, Leeds. Works No **832** of 1903 this engine was also retired to the Darley Dale Yard by 1937, but was retained by Lehane, Mackenzie & Shand Ltd., and seen at work at Scapa Flow in 1943. The age of the small industrial type of locomotive on public works contracts and similar projects was declining after the end of World War II as was the demand for 'navvies' as mechanised earth moving plant of huge proportions and capacities became available and *Brownhill* was scrapped in 1951. **J.Peden collection**

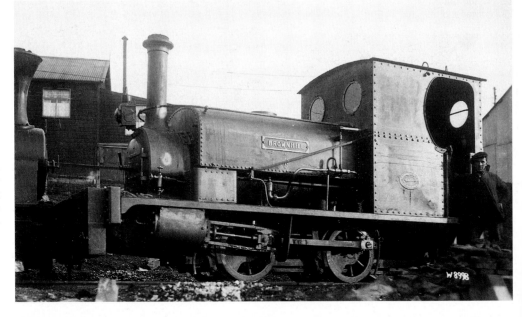

ALONGSIDE FERNILEE RESERVOIR

Continuing from page 15, the site of the Gunpowder works is still on the right beneath the waters of Fernilee Reservoir.

Turning round, the photographer is looking northwards towards Whaley Bridge and the site of the Gunpowder works is now to the left.

Fernilee, former route of the C&HPR May 1998: Two robust stone gate-posts on the bank mark a point where a farm-track or by-road crossed the line of the railway at right angles. The direction is looking north towards Shallcross Incline and Whaley Bridge.

Fernilee Bridleway. May 1998: From the top of Shallcross Incline the abandoned route of the C&HPR ran on the level for nearly two miles along the eastern slope of the Goyt Valley. This view looking south is between the spot where a quarry was opened by the contractors Lehane Mackenzie & Shand on the lands of Upper Mill Farm and the foot of the former Bunsall Incline.

Less vegetation clothes the slopes as the walker proceeds southwards and this prospect is seen on turning to face Whaley Bridge; the site of the Gunpowder works is now distant just to the left of an outcrop which can hardly be distinguished from this point.

This view across Fernilee Reservoir has Whaley Bridge to the left and Cromford to the right. The scene however does not relate to the fact that the Whaley to Buxton road (Long Hill) runs but a short distance above the shores of the reservoir to the right.

Fernilee Reservoir May 1998: Mrs. Jacqueline Fox beside Fernilee Reservoir walking along the Bridleway on the former railway route towards the foot of the legendary Bunsall Incline. The high embankment crossing the picture is the dam of the Errwood Reservoir built (1964 - 1968)   ***Photographs G.K.Fox***

Goyt Valley. May 1998: A view taken from the top of the Errwood Dam, looking towards Whaley Bridge of the Fernilee Reservoir, the former original route of the Cromford & High Peak Railway following the right hand shoreline. *G.K.Fox*

Bunsall Incline: On this plateau the two original inclines met and wagons were transferred between the upper and lower chains until 6 June 1857 when the inclines were combined. About ninety years later the ruins of the engineman's house on the right was demolished, but some stone sleeper blocks may still be seen. *Dr.J.R.Hollick*

May 1978 near the site above stands this commemorative plaque presented by the Stephenson Locomotive Society in 1972 and dedicated 7 January 1973. *G.K.Fox*

Bunsall Incline: An evocative scene looking down the abandoned incline towards its foot, with Bridge No 57, in the distance. Trains being hauled up this one-time double-incline had another 29 miles 24 chains of wild country to traverse before arriving at Cromford Wharf. *Dr.J.R.Hollick*

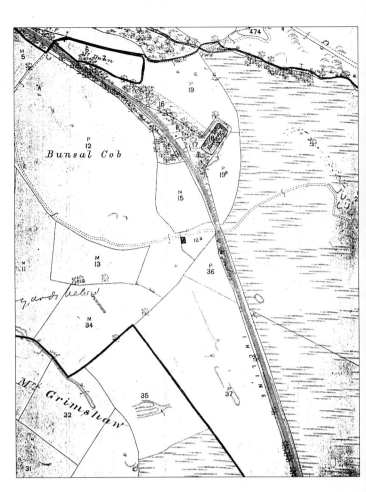

Bunsall. May 1998: Looking north, down the road by which motorists may now ascend the former C&HPR incline, the 1930's built Fernilee Reservoir is seen off centre, and the site of Shallcross & Whaley Bridge beyond. *G.K.Fox*

Bunsall. Another view taken from near the top of Bunsall before its transformation into the metalled highway featured above centre. Fernilee Reservoir may be seen in the distance. *Dr.J.R.Hollick*

From the top of the incline there is a fine view with the Fernilee reservoir dominating. Continuing on, the remains of the intermediate stationary engine house and reservoir may be seen and there is a stone monument, with an inscribed plaque, dedicated on 7 January 1973, to the former incline, presented by the Stephenson Locomotive Society in 1972. The area once Shallcross Yard is now occupied by 'Cromford Court' a complex of old people's homes, but the base of the old crane remains, also one or two warning notices. Beyond this the local council has converted the former C&HPR track into a linear park, at its commencement is a circular plaque bearing a replica of the C&HPR seal. It is mounted in a circular stone surround beneath which is one of the original cast-iron, fish-bellied rails.

Ladmanlow station was closed in 1954, and the level crossing was removed in 1958, the well known wrought iron plate-girder skew bridge over the A54, Buxton - Macclesfield road (renewed in 1865) was dismantled in 1958. An underground telecommunications cable runs through Burbage tunnel, stone lined throughout it now has a locked door at each end. Continuing onwards from the north side, the site of a former level crossing of the C&HPR track becomes part of the service road built in 1966 in connection with the construction of the Errwood reservoir.

Bunsall. Early 1930's: This scene shows the ruins (now demolished) of the former Bunsall Top engine house. *Dr.J.R.Hollick*

Bunsall to Burbage Tunnel & Ladmanlow: This is the scenery that Edward Bradbury enjoyed on his 1880 footplate trip. *Dr.J.R.Hollick*

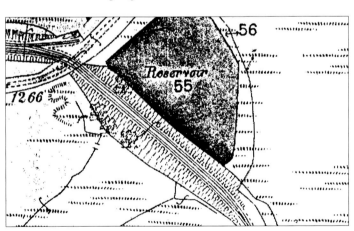

September 1998: The old (1831) railway embankment depicted in this view formed a dam for the Bunsall top reservoir, (above) which supplied water for the stationary engines and locomotive purposes. *G.K.Fox*

Above and Right - Lower: These two views vividly portray the route of the old C&HPR over the aptly named Wildmoor. The lower opposite view is looking towards Bunsall whilst in the lower scene the photographer was looking towards the northern portal of Burbage tunnel.
Both L.M.Hobdey

FROM WHALEY BRIDGE TO CROMFORD WHARF AND HIGH PEAK JUNCTION

Details of the train known as THE 'FLY ' taken from our copy of the Working Timetable published as "November 1877 until further notice." indicate that in fact the term was applied to the working of three trains: No 5 from Whaley Bridge to Ladmanlow, No 6 from Ladmanlow to Hurdlow (Foot of) and No 7 from Hurdlow to Cromford, where it was booked to arrive at 12.15 pm.

WHALEY BRIDGE (Incline No 9)
SHALLCROSS (Incline No 8)

Whaley Bridge in 1876 does not appear to have been the most salubrious of locations, the landscape was reportedly scarred with mines and pits, colliery gins and slag heaps, and small works and factories proliferated, but that was where the 'Fly' began its journey, its booked departure time being 7.10 am and any passengers would undertake the first 'leg' of their journey riding in the guard's "break" van, proceeding then as part of a 'run' hauled up the Shallcross Gradient, described as a straight rise at 1 in 8·5, over a double line of railway, worked by an endless chain, and stationary engine.

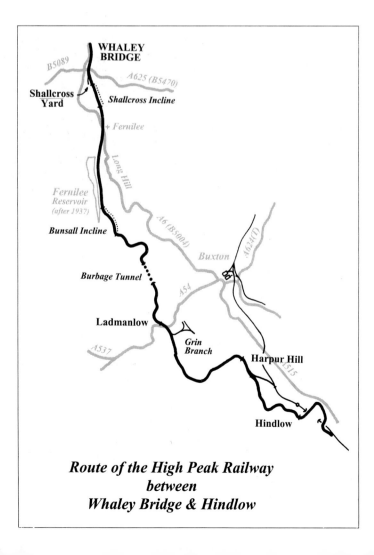

***Route of the High Peak Railway
between
Whaley Bridge & Hindlow***

THE GOYT VALLEY & BUNSALL
Double Incline No 6 and No 7)

From Shallcross the C&HPR next entered upon typical moorland scenery beside the River Goyt, the railway on the eastern side of the valley with the engine probably working tender first. Train No 5 was timed to arrive at Bunsall, (Top of) 4 miles from Whaley Bridge at 8 am, but the route had afforded also a delightful prospect of the wooded shade of Errwood Hall, at a point where the line was terraced above the Goyt Valley, on the approach to Bunsall, although it is doubtful that this view would be appreciated by the engine-men on their open footplate. The engine 'came off,' at the foot of the ascent, and the train was split to be worked up the Bunsall inclines, which are described as being 'double,' with the first incline straight, and the second on the curve.(This location Dr Hollick describes as "now the new Goyt Valley road").

BUNSALL INCLINE (TOP OF)
- BURBAGE TUNNEL

The train on leaving Bunsall (Top of), then encountered another expanse of moorland terrain, where the romantically inclined might wax lyrical at the sight of heather growing to the very edge of the line, the keen, fresh air, and the sight of wild grouse, or curlew, rising on the approach of the train. The splendour of Buxton's Victorian villas, was seen below on the left, as the train approached Burbage Tunnel, a 580 yard bore through the rock. (The tunnel was abandoned, as was the combined Bunsall Incline on the section north of Ladmanlow, on 25 June 1892, when the new line from Hurdlow to Buxton was opened).

J. B. FELL AND THE TRIALS OF HIS CENTRE RAIL SYSTEM for the proposed Mont Cenis Pass railway

In his definitive volume 'The British Steam Locomotive 1825-1925, the late E. L. Ahrons in referring to the engine built for Mr J. B. FELL to his patented central rail system by Brassey & Co., of the Canada Works, Birkenhead in 1863 states that it was tried out "on a track, 800 yards long of 3 ft 7³/₈ in. gauge laid on a gradient of 1 in 13·5 on the High Peak Railway, in Derbyshire". Some authorities consider that these trials possibly took place alongside, or near the site of the Hopton Incline, although in the relevant period, 1863 - 1864, the Whaley Bridge Incline was being reconstructed, and it now seems more probable that the Fell system was tried out on two comparatively short inclines of 180 yds and 150 yds, with gradients of 1 in 13·5 and 1 in 12 respectively at Whaley.

A scene typical of the inhospitable terrain c.1968: between Bunsall Top and the northern face of the Burbage Tunnel *L.M.Hobdey*

Burbage Tunnel - Northern Portal c.1968: The tunnel mouth looks singularly uninviting - small wonder that Edward Bradbury was overwhelmed during his foot-plate experience. *L.M.Hobdey*

Burbage Tunnel c.1968: The abandoned portal in close-up certainly appeared grim, foreboding, even dangerous to the explorer of the route of the former Cromford & High Peak Railway, but the local sheep had no such qualms, taking shelter from inclement conditions and wandering in and out at will. *L.M.Hobdey*

Burbage Tunnel - Southern Portal: with Tunnel Farm in the upper left of the picture. Photo taken before the tunnel mouth was bricked up. *L.M.Hobdey*

Edge Moor: Still spanning the open moor as straight as a Roman road, the former route of the abandoned railway is now flanked by the dry-stone walls so associated with this type of terrain.

C&HPR: 'Straight as a ruler' is this section of the abandoned track bed flanked by enroaching bushes in its crossing of Edge Moor.

The old Turnpike Road: The photographer was looking towards Colliery Junction (see following pages) when he took this picture of the bridge which carried the old Buxton road over the Cromford & High Peak Railway track bed. *Mr L. M. Hobdey took all the pictures that feature on this page on one of his extensive explorations of the line in the late 1950's and early 1960's.*

Colliery Junction. 1948: This view of Bridge No 54 was taken in what were quite normal winter weather conditions at this period, with snow on the ground and judging by the lowering skies quite a lot more to come. The line terminated here after 1892, when the section towards Shallcross Sidings, and Whaley Bridge was dispensed with on the opening of the new Buxton - Hurdlow - Harpur Hill sections. So far as the abandoned section is concerned any photographs that might have been taken whilst it was in operation seem to have disappeared. ***Photographs L.M.Hobdey***

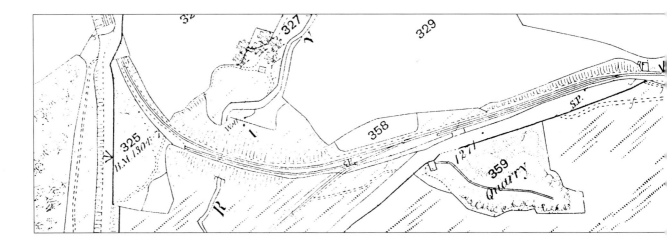

Ladmanlow: 'The Good Old Days'. Looking almost like a model railway layout in their variety of type and livery is this amazing collection of wagons, cattle trucks, and vans, the historian or railway modeller could spend hours poring over this masterpiece by some turn of the century photographer, with a powerful glass picking out a wealth of hidden detail.   ***Basil Jeuda collection***

Ladmanlow. 29 April 1955: In this picture, Bridge No 54 - still in existence but in filled in 1974 - appears far right carrying the 'old' road to Macclesfield across the track bed and in the foreground is a close-up view of the site of Colliery Junction terminating in a rather crude stop-block. With further reference to veteran photographers, a Mr C. M. Doncaster travelled to the High Peak from his home at Totley and took pictures known to have covered operations as far as Ladmanlow Yard but nothing is known beyond that. A few pictures exist of mines in the area but none showing the full extent of High Peak industrial activity here.   ***Harry Townley***

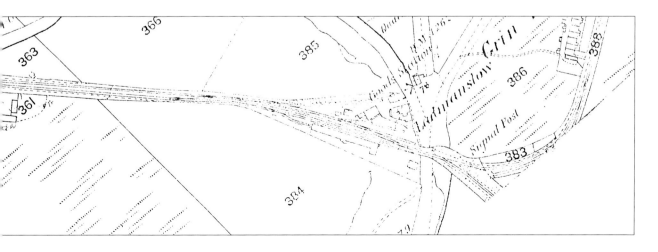

Accidents - Dangerous Operating Practices on the C&HPR as recorded in this account of a head-on collision between Ladmanlow and Harpur Hill.
Board of Trade, (Railway Department)

EXTRACT BEGINS Whitehall, 15th February 1876.

"Sir, I have the honour to report, for the information of the Board of Trade, in compliance with the instructions contained in your order of the 14th ultimo, the result of my inquiry into the circumstances which attended a collision that occurred on the 17th December, between Ladmanlow and Harpur Hill, on the Cromford and High Peak Railway, between two mineral trains travelling in opposite directions.

The fireman of one of the engines (George Tumington) was unfortunately killed, the driver (William Chappell) had his thigh fractured, and the driver and fireman of the other engine are returned as "slightly shaken" whilst the two engines were a good deal damaged, and eight wagons to a less extent.

The Cromford and High Peak Railway is connected at its two extremities, with the London and North Western Railway at Whaley Bridge, and with the Midland Railway at Cromford. The traffic up certain inclines is worked by stationary engines, but on the high table-land on which the larger portion of the whole length of the line has been constructed it is now worked by locomotive power. Formerly it was nothing more than a tramway, and it is still considered as a mineral line, although I understand, a very small amount of passenger traffic is carried on it, in an exceptional manner, by a very limited number of trains, without the issue of tickets to the passengers.

It is 33.5 miles in length, and is now leased in perpetuity to the London and North-Western Railway Company. It is single throughout, with sidings at various places, and the arrangements of signals and for working the traffic are different from any that I have met with over any other part of the London and North Western Railway.

The "time-table" for the Cromford and High Peak Railway for April 1874, and until further orders," contained the particulars relating to 51 trains running in each direction, and at the foot of this time table the following "regulations for working between Ladmanlow and Harpur Hill" are given.

"The line between Ladmanlow and Harpur Hill must be worked by an engine staff, lettered L. and H.H. All engines passing between these points must carry the staff, with the exception of the 5.0 am and 10.55 am trains from Ladmanlow and the 10.15 am and 3.15 pm trains from Harpur Hill. The engine-men in charge of these four trains must see the staff at the starting points immediately before proceeding on their journey. At Ladmanlow, between the Lime Company's Branch and the coal siding, the line must be worked by signals from Ladmanlow, and engines must not pass over this length at a greater speed than four miles an hour. The arm on that side of the signal-post which is nearest to the main line of rails is the signal for engines from Whaley Bridge to Cromford, or Cromford to Whaley Bridge. The arm on the side of the signal-post away from the main line is the signal for engines between Ladmanlow and the coal branch. An engineman from the main line must give one whistle, and from the branch or coal siding two whistles, and must not proceed beyond the signal until it is lowered."

The last time-table that was issued was for "October 1875, and until further notice," and it has not been followed by any other. It related to 15 trains running in each direction, but the preceding regulations for working between Ladmanlow and Harpur are omitted at the foot of the table.

Ladmanlow is distant about 2.5 miles from Harpur Hill. The traffic on this part of the Cromford and High Peak Railway is worked in the following manner: One locomotive engine works the traffic over the single line between Ladmanlow and Harpur, and a second locomotive engine works the long traffic between Ladmanlow and Hopton, 21.5 miles apart, also passing over the portion of single line between Ladmanlow and Harpur Hill, and the trains which pass over this long length are called fly trains. There is a station master at Ladmanlow, but none at Harpur Hill.

The evidence of the company's servants who could afford any information respecting the collision is as follows :

William Chappell, driver of engine No 1835 states "that he has been an engine-driver for 17 years, and driving all that time on the Cromford and High Peak Railway; that on the morning on which the collision occurred he had to take a train consisting of an engine and 14 waggons, from Ladmanlow to Hopton, and he left Ladmanlow about 9.0 am although his proper time for starting was 8.30 am, and when he had gone about a mile on the way he came into collision with a goods train loaded with lime (which was travelling in the opposite direction from Harpur Hill to Ladmanlow) on the same line of rails as he was running on: that he judged he was going at about 10 miles an hour, but he could form no idea of the rate at which the other train was travelling towards him: that there was a heavy mist hanging about that morning and he could not see above 10 yards in front of him: that, previous to leaving Ladmanlow, he had stopped his train at the Leek Road level crossing, so that the break-van might be opposite to the station-master's hut to allow the guard to unload some things; and the semaphore-signal was off when he first started, and his engine had passed the level crossing when he stopped nearly opposite to the signal, and when the guard had finished his work he gave a signal for him to proceed: that there were only two engines that worked over the line, and one of them (Goodwin's) had left Ladmanlow before him, but he did not know it at the time, and he had since been told that Goodwin, the driver of the other engine had the 'engine staff': he also said that when one engine was going on the line the driver had to take the 'staff' which guaranteed a clear line, according to the regulations of the company, and the 'staff' would be retained by the driver till he returned; but when the other engine was in the station he did not take the 'staff:' that he had not made any inquiry with regard to the 'staff' or as to whether Goodwin's engine was in the station, and he came to the conclusion that Goodwin was in the station-siding, as he had seen him some time before take his engine there, and when he started from Ladmanlow along the line to Harpur Hill he did so in the full belief that Goodwin was behind him: that there was no person appointed to give the 'staff' to the engine-drivers, but they simply handed it from one to the other: that when leaving the crossing at the Leek Road he did not notice the semaphore-signal, but saw the guard, from whom he got the signal to start, but he admits that he did not whistle for the signal to be taken off. He also stated that when he commenced working over the length between Ladmanlow and Hopton on the 30th March 1872: that there was no rule at the bottom of the time tables in 1872 which required that he should either have or see the 'staff' before leaving Ladmanlow or Harpur Hill, at least he does not recollect any rule, but in 1873 the rule was introduced at the bottom of the time-table, and he is furnished with copies of the time-tables whenever changes are made in them: that he does not work the local trains, but merely the through trains between Ladmanlow and Hopton, and more frequently carries the 'staff' than he leaves it behind: that when he and the driver of the local train between Ladmanlow and Harpur Hill, are at either of these places at the same time he would not look for the 'staff' if he saw the engine, but leave before the other train: that the reason why he did not look for the staff on the 17th December was that he believed he was going to leave before the other train about 10 minutes before 9 o'clock or thereabouts: that he does not consider that there has been any alteration in the mode of working sanctioned, caused by the omission of the rules about the 'staff' in the time table for October 1875, which changes the hours of the trains: that he did not that morning go into the station-master's hut to enter the time of his leaving, and the entry of 9.0 in that book is not his entry: that he did not make any entry anywhere of the time of his starting that morning: that he did not about 8.30 am hear Goodwin's engine whistle, as he was at that time in the shed, and after that he went to his lodgings at the gatekeeper's house: that he did not stop five minutes after drawing up opposite to the semaphore-signal, and did not see the station-master that morning after 6.0 am nor his boy; and that he was hurt by the collision, and has not been at work since it occurred."

George Goodwin engine-driver for 14 years, states "that he left Ladmanlow for Harpur Hill with a train of waggons for Harpur Hill, a little before 6.0 am, and left Harpur Hill for Ladmanlow about 7.0 am; after having discharged the trucks he had brought from Ladmanlow; that he next left Ladmanlow for Harpur Hill about 8.30 am, and, before leaving the station, he had seen another engine there, of which William Chappell was the driver, and when he first saw Chappell he was oiling his engine, and seemed to look up, but did not make any sign of recognition, and when he passed Chappell's engine there would not be more than 12 yards between them; that before he left the station he noticed the semaphore-signal, which was on at 'danger' against him, and he gave the usual signal to the station-master by whistling, and the signal, which is worked by the station-master or his assistant, was altered so as to allow him to pass; that at times when the station-master is not in the office where the signal is worked, permission to go is given by a wave of the hand, and he had, under these circumstances, passed on when the semaphore-signal has been against him: that there is a 'staff' given to the engine-driver which gives him entire control over the line during the time that he has it in his possession, and he had it in his possession, and took it to Harpur Hill, when he left about 8.30 am, and, therefore, thought he was perfectly safe on the line: that it was a rule that an engine-driver, previous to leaving the station, should see that the 'staff' was at that end of the line, and it has not to his knowledge been the habit of the drivers to go without it, and at the end of each journey it should be taken into the office of the station-master, and kept there until wanted again: but in practice the 'staff' is taken into the station-master's office at night, and not at the end of each journey: that on the morning in question the 'staff' was not in the station-master's office, owing to the fact that another driver had not delivered it there the previous night, and he had obtained it from the other driver: that when any of the drivers had to go on a journey they had to book the time when the train starts, as also the number of waggons there are on the train, and his son, who was with him on the engine, had done so that morning: that he believes he has always had the 'staff' with him in his journeys to and from Ladmanlow and Harpur Hill, and he has always worked over this length, but formerly he worked beyond Harpur Hill: that in the return journey from Harpur Hill, between 8.30 and 9.0 am, with 13 lime waggons on, he was running engine first, and when he had traversed about half the distance he met another engine on the same line of rails, when he was going at the rate of 12 or 13 miles an hour, and his engine mounted on the tender of the other engine, which was running tender first: that it was so very foggy that he does not think he was more than 10 or 12 yards from the other engine when he first saw it, and he had no time to do anything before the collision took place, about 9 a.m :that he was slightly hurt about the shoulders, and laid up for one day."

George William Goodwin, son of the engine-driver states" that on the 17th December he was on the engine driven by his father, and acting as his fireman: that they left Ladmanlow at 8.30 am, with an engine and nine empty waggons, but before leaving the station his father whistled for the signal to drop, and it was done, and they passed on, that there was a 'staff' which his father received before leaving, according to the rules of the Company: that he saw the station-master in his office when he went to book the train out at 8.25 am, or 8.30: that the station-master left the office to remove the signal when he heard the whistle from the engine, but he does not know who dropped the signal, and when this was done he joined his father, and proceeded with the train to Harpur Hill: that in returning from Harpur Hill to Ladmanlow, when about half-way between those places, they met another engine, and came into violent collision with it, and both were thrown off the line: that they were running as near as he could say, about 12 or 13 miles an hour when the collision occurred: that he saw no-one but his father before the collision, and could only see about 60 yards in front, and had only time to say 'See he's coming' then jumped off, and had only just reached the ground when the smash occurred: that when he spoke, his father turned round, but had not time to jump: that the tender of the other engine was thrown down the bank, and soon afterwards he saw the fireman of the other engine fast on the outside wheel of his own engine, head downwards, and the other engine on him, but he was then dead: that they always take the 'staff' with them, but never start on merely seeing it: that his father's train always follows the fly train when both are at Ladmanlow or Harpur Hill: that the engine of the fly train was at Ladmanlow on the 17th December at 8.30 am, but the fly train from Bunsall had not arrived at Ladmanlow at that time: that he had never passed the semaphore when it was against their leaving the station, except the first thing in the morning, when the semaphore was frozen, and only when the station-master gave consent: that the reason his father took the 'staff' from another engine-driver instead of the station-master's office was on account of the other driver having worked the line on the night before, and not having delivered the 'staff' up to the station-master's office: that he and his father had been working the Bunsall line the day before, and had changed that morning: that he had been a fireman about three months."

James Wardle, station-master at Ladmanlow, states that he was at the station on the morning of the accident, and saw the train driven by Goodwin in the station about 8.0 am, but was not in the station when Goodwin left at 8.30 am, and does not remember seeing Goodwin's son till after the accident had occurred: that Goodwin had made a journey to Harpur Hill and back on the same morning, having set off the first time at 5.35 am, : that Goodwin went into the office and told him that he had left the lime, which he should have brought from Harpur Hill, on the advice of the foreman, because he had no empty trucks to put in place of those to be brought away: and the second journey made by Goodwin was an extra one, on account of his having left the waggons of lime behind him, and Chappell might not have known that Goodwin was on the line: that Goodwin had been in the siding for some empties, and if Chappell was on his engine he could not have missed seeing Goodwin come out of the siding on his second journey to Harpur Hill: that there is no regularity in the departure of the engines, and there sometimes occurred a difference of half an hour either late or soon: that he does not know whether the signal was taken off for Goodwin to leave about 8.30 am, but the boy states that it was: that he got back to the station from his breakfast about 10 minutes before 9.00am, and Chappell had not left at that time: that he did not hear Chappell whistle that morning for the signal, and he would not be above 25 yards from where he was: that he believes Chappell had not been in the office to record the time of his leaving: that he did not give Chappell permission to leave that morning, and did not know that he had left before the accident occurred, and that it is not the practice for trains to leave without getting his or the guard's permission, and he would have reported any driver who left without permission: that Chappell should either have got the 'staff' or have seen it before leaving that morning: that the staff is generally kept in the engine shed at night, and the driver usually fetches it from his office, or the shed, for the first trip in the morning, when it has been left there overnight: that he does not recollect a case in which, when the Harpur Hill and the fly train are both at Ladmanlow station at the same time, of the Harpur Hill train leaving before the fly train: that the drivers do not, as a rule, enter the times when they leave Ladmanlow in the engine-driver's time book: that Goodwin's first trip was not entered before his train started, as the office was not open: that he cannot say whether the second trip was entered before he left or not, but the entries in the time book are as follows:

'Goodwin left for the first trip at 5.37, and returned at 6.52. 'Second trip left at 8.23.'

'That he does not know whether Chappell's first trip was entered before he left or not. The entry is at 9 am He said there was no rule that the staff should be deposited with him.'"

James W. Wardle, the son of the station-master, 14 years of age, states" that he assists his father and had been engaged in doing so for seven weeks when the accident occurred: that he recollects the 17th December, and got to the office between 7 am, and 7.30 am, and lowered the signal for Goodwin's train between 8 and 8.30 am, and he put the signal up after that train had gone: that he was at his breakfast when the fly train left, and did not see it go, and when he came from his breakfast both signals were up: that when both trains are at the station together, the fly train goes first, and he has never known the Harpur Hill train to go before the fly train.

Joseph Goddard, in charge of the gates at the level-crossing on the Leek Road, states "that after Goodwin left at 8.23 the semaphore signal was put up by someone and never taken off again before Chappell left: that he recollected Chappell coming up to the points, which he turned for the driver to go on the main-line, when the stoker who was killed told him that they were ready: that Chappell did not whistle, and he believed the semaphore signal was not lowered: that he saw the guard give the driver a signal to proceed, and Chappell went on at once: that he had been in the employ of the company since 1861: that he knew that Goodwin had gone to Harpur Hill within 35 minutes of that time, and he had never known Goodwin to return again as on this occasion: That he knew they often waited for each other at Harpur Hill and he never knew Goodwin return again before Chappell had passed: that it has been the practice for the fly train to proceed when the semaphore has not been taken off, sometimes it is lowered, and sometimes not: that he has never known the fly train to proceed without a signal from the guard: that sometimes the fly train would leave before the Harpur Hill train, and sometimes afterwards, when both are at the station together: that he has seen either the driver or the fireman of the Harpur Hill train engine hand the 'staff' to the fly train engine: that he has seen this frequently done by the men working the Harpur Hill train, but he could not say distinctly that he has seen Goodwin do this: that he entered the 8.23 in the engine-driver's time-book as soon as Goodwin's train left, and he does not think the semaphore signal could have been lowered without his knowing it."

John Melbourne, guard of the train driven by Chappell, states "that they left at 9.00am instead of 8.30 am, but it was a regular thing for them to be that time late: that he noticed another engine in the station, driven by John Lupton, before he left, but he saw no other: that he had not seen Goodwin's engine in the station that morning, and he did not know that Goodwin had gone on to Harpur Hill: that he gave out two parcels to the station-master when Chappell had drawn the train ahead so as to bring his van opposite to the station-master's hut; that he gave one of these parcels to John Lupton, and the other was received by the station-master: that Lupton's engine was in the steam-shed siding at that time, and he did not take anything from the station-master's hut; that he did not obtain the signal and did not whistle, nor give Chappell any signal to start that day: that at the departure side of the station there is a semaphore to signal trains in and out, and the station-master uses it, but it was not used, to his knowledge, to let out his train: that he did not look at it because he was occupied counting the waggons: that the fog was very thick, so that you could not see the length of the train, and he could not say whether the signal was up or down: that no signal was given for the train to go on, as he had previously told Chappell that he had two parcels to give out, and that there was nothing to come out of the station-master's hut: that they had no right to leave the station before the semaphore was lowered, and he never missed noticing the semaphore, to his knowledge, except on this occasion: that there was no signal from the station-master, and he thought that he was aware that the train was going on, but he might have thought that they were going to stop before leaving the station: that they moved steadily from Ladmanlow station with the speed gradually increasing till the time of the accident: that there was a 'staff' which they had to use, so that no train could foul another, and he was of the opinion that the 'staff' was in Chappell's possession, but it was not, and without that 'staff' Chappell had no right to go, but it was not his duty to inquire whether the 'staff' was on the train or not, as the guard never 'interferes' with the 'staff': that he never heard of any train travelling on the line without the 'staff' from the station and if he had known it he would not have gone: that the station-master is the responsible person as to the passing of the trains in and out, and every time an engine goes out of the station the semaphore ought to be dropped: that they often started at 9 o'clock because they could not get from Whaley Bridge to Ladmanlow by 8.30 am, the time they ought to start: that the goods manager at Cromford and the locomotive inspector knew this for some time past."

James Wardle, engine-cleaner states "that he saw Chappell approaching the crossing when the signal was at stop: that he was stopping at the shed next the crossing, perhaps 10 or 12 yards from it: that he (Chappell) did not whistle as he approached the crossing, and engines are not allowed to pass without whistling: that Chappell did not stop after passing the crossing, but kept on going on,"

I have thought it desirable to give the whole of the evidence relating to this collision, as there is a good deal that is contradictory in it, and the more so, as it discloses a very loose system of working the traffic.

But I gathered from the evidence of the men, taken in connection with the time table of the trains, that the general practice has been for the train which runs the long distance from Ladmanlow to Hopton (21·5 miles), or as it is called by the men, the fly train, when it and the local train to Harpur Hill are at Ladmanlow at the same time, for the fly train to leave first, when the driver might sometimes see the staff, but at all events would see the engine of the local train, and the staff would then be carried by the following local train engine. But on this particular morning the local trip had been from Ladmanlow to Harpur Hill early in the morning, and had not brought back some waggons of lime which were required when it returned just before 7 o'clock. It does not appear whether the driver of the local train was directed to go back for those waggons, but it is certain that he went back to Harpur Hill unknown to Chappell, the driver of the fly train, who imagined that he was still at Ladmanlow, when he (Chappell) started a little before 9 o'clock.

The collision was the undoubted result of the neglect of Chappell, in having failed to obey that portion of the rule printed below the April time table of the year 1874, which requires the drivers of four of the local trains, which are specially named, to see the staff at the starting points before proceeding on their journey, the three first-named trains being apparently fly trains, while the last train does not appear in that table at all.

But there does not appear to be any question that the drivers of the local and fly trains perfectly understood that they were either to have the staff in their possession or see it before starting from Ladmanlow; but Chappell was apparently misled by Goodwin's going back from Ladmanlow to Harpur Hill with the local train five minutes before the appointed time for him to leave.

The London and North Western Railway Company were, I believe, the first to introduce and to make use of the train staff and ticket system for the working of single lines, which, if strictly upheld, certainly must prevent collisions from taking place between trains travelling in opposite directions; and I certainly was very much surprised to find that the general regulations of the company, and those which they introduced for the working of single lines, were not in use at all on the Cromford and High Peak Railway, now exclusively under their control and management.

It is quite true that, from the nature of the ground, if it had been a clear day, the probability is that this infringement of the regulations would not have led to any collision, as the engines could have been seen at a very considerable distance from each other.

If, as I was informed, the London and North-Western Railway Company permit passengers to be carried by some of their trains (and I have no doubt of this being a great boon to the residents), I should imagine that it would be proper for the company to submit their line to the Board of Trade, that it might be inspected in accordance with the various Acts of Parliament which were in force long before they obtained the lease of this line. (see Section 77 of the Cromford and High Peak Railway Act, 1855)*"

> I have, &c,
> **W.Yolland**
> **Colonel**
> **The Secretary,**
> **(Railway Department)**
> **Board of Trade.**

*Section 77: " That after the passing of this Act no portion of the railway shall be deemed to have been opened for the public conveyance of passengers, but the said railway shall be subject to the provisions of the act of the fifth and sixth years of the reign of Her present Majesty, Chapter fifty-five, intituled An Act for the better Regulation of Railways, and for the Conveyance of Troops, in the same manner as if the railway had been constructed under the powers of this Act.

Printed copies of the report were sent to the Company on 7th March 1876

We, (your authors) have included the Inspecting Officer's report of the foregoing incident in full, as it shows exactly how the northern end of the High Peak line was being worked in the mid 1870's and my colleague and former foot-plateman Mike Bentley, who knows the line intimately from his days at Buxton Shed (see SCENES FROM THE PAST: 24 BUXTON ENGINES AND MEN) has 'read between the lines' of the report and compiled the enlightening résumé that follows:

The report gives an intriguing insight into that remote world, into which very few officials ever ventured, although it was only 30-35 miles away from the centre of the London & North Western Railway system at Crewe. It is quite obvious that when the LNWR authorities took over the High Peak line no effort was made to introduce a more up to date and efficient method of working than had existed prior to their advent. Let us now look at Colonel Yolland's report in detail, and 'read between the lines' for that is where the real truth of the climate of events that led to this accident are to be found.

FIRSTLY the locomotives. Three were employed daily at this time, Driver Chappell had Crewe Goods 2-4-0 No 1835 which had just been renumbered in May of 1875; it had formerly been No 170 and, when it first arrived at Ladmanlow on 2nd December 1869 was named *Candidate*, the name being removed in 1872.

Driver Goodwin, even though the report fails to mention his locomotive probably had the other Crewe Goods 2-4-0, No 1848 this also had been renumbered in May of 1875, and was originally No 172 *Admiral* on its arrival at Ladmanlow on 18 May 1870; it lost its name on 8 October 1873.

Driver Lupton who was working the Ladmanlow to Bunsall Top section would possibly have had C&HPR No 7, by now carrying the LNWR No 1946, one of the two Vulcan Foundry 0-6-0 tanks with outside cylinders, this and its sister loco No 6 were delivered new to Ladmanlow in March and April 1860 when horses were finally removed from wagon haulage on this section. It had been found advantageous to replace the two C&HPR locomotives on the run to Hopton Top, 21·5 miles, by using Crewe goods tender locos, with their greater coal and water capacity.

Now to examine the circumstances leading to the accident: In the evidence given by George William Goodwin, fireman to his father George Goodwin, he states that he and his father had been working the Bunsall section the previous day, and this was their first day back on the Harpur Hill section, so it is obvious that Drivers Goodwin and Lupton worked turn about on the local jobs, whilst Chappell, the senior man worked to Hopton exclusively.

The first mistake appears to have been made by the previous days Harpur Hill crew, the requirement of empties for one of the Harpur Hill Quarries had been "forgotten" in the change-over, so when Goodwin arrived to remove the 13 loaded wagons, he had no empties to place in position for the 6.00am quarry loading gang to fill; the nine empties they had brought were undoubtedly for a loading gang at one of the other quarries. The local foreman, be he quarry or railway employed, would not be amused, as he would in this instance, have a gang of men standing idle, with nothing to load. So, realising that their failure to bring sufficient wagons up (although not their -Goodwin's-fault) would probably mean trouble for Lupton's crew, Driver Goodwin returned to Ladmanlow to 'knock out' another train of empties, however he would not have taken this action 'off his own bat' but would be acting on instructions. One can understand the foreman at Harpur Hill demanding this action, as Goodwin's next booked trip to Harpur Hill was not until after the passage of the **'Fly'** to Hopton, so the 'loading gang' would have been standing around until 9.00am at least.

Back at Ladmanlow Driver Chappell was oiling No 1835 on the shed road. Lupton would be starting away from Bunsall Top with the Hopton train which was to be taken over by Chappell, and anyone who has worked, or lived, in the High Peak area, especially around Axe Edge above Ladmanlow will know only too well what thick mist really means; so, with no lights in the yard, or from the nearby houses (the common form of lighting at the time would be oil lamps or candles) men and locomotives would move around 'like ghosts,' sight and sound being muffled almost to the point of extinction. Driver Goodwin states he passed within 12 yards of where Chappell was oiling his loco, Chappell looked but made no acknowledgement; he may well have thought it was Driver Goodwin getting his normal second trip ready for his departure after the **'Fly.'**

Driver Goodwin departed at 8.23am (from Ladmanlow) with the badly needed empties, on arrival at Harpur Hill he would draw out the loaded wagons and replace them with the empties. The loaded wagons would be intended for Whaley Bridge, and Goodwin would know that they would have to be at Ladmanlow ready for Driver Lupton's next trip back to Bunsall, so he certainly would 'get stuck in' to get back to Ladmanlow quickly without delaying the departure of the **'Fly.'** Throughout this operation Driver Goodwin was in possession of the 'Train Staff' and was therefore carrying out his job correctly. The estimated speeds of the trains at the point of collision must be taken 'with a pinch of salt.' Working in heavy mist is one of the most difficult tasks drivers of locomotive engines (or motor vehicles) have to do; both engines involved were cab-less, and all engines on the High Peak railway faced towards Whaley Bridge, so Driver Chappell was running tender first, and 30 minutes late, so he too, would be moving his train along smartly. Driver Goodwin, trying to minimise delay to the **'Fly'** would also be moving briskly, each probably doing between 15 to 20 mph resulting in an impact speed at the time of the collision of 30 to 40 mph .the weight of the trains of course being an added factor.

Poor Fireman Tumington was probably working on the shovel when the impact occurred, and when the tender of his locomotive was thrown sideways he would fall between the engine and tender and was probably run over by the trailing driving wheels of his engine, No 1835 must also have turned over, as his body was found 'draped' over the wheel, with the front end of Goodwin's engine pinning him there.

For all concerned the collision must have been a dreadful shock, still barely daylight at the time, and taking place in a swirling thick mist, the sort of horrific railway accident, instilling the same sort of emotions in staff as do those mishaps sustained in tunnels.

However, having studied this aspect of events let us return to Ladmanlow and review the events relating to Driver Chappell's departure. Chappell had taken over the 14 wagon train brought by Driver Lupton from Bunsall, which had a passenger, or passengers in the **'Fly'** brake van; he drew up to allow his guard to unload parcels at the Station-master's cabin and should have heard Lupton's engine, which by now was on the Shed road, getting water and preparing generally, and yet he was still under the impression that Goodwin was in the yard; he states his guard, John Melbourne gave him the 'tip' to go. This statement is verified by the evidence of the Crossing Keeper, Joseph Goddard, who stated that he saw the Guard give the signal for the train to proceed, all denied by Guard Melbourne. Then the crucial event took place, Driver Chappell in accordance with his usual practice departed, without a care in the world! because he believed that '"the Fly always departed before the 'tripper' to Harpur Hill".

Stationmaster Wardle also declared that this was always the case, yet Crossing Keeper Goddard, (who seems to have had more knowledge of the appropriate Rules and Regulations than anyone else) was not so sure, he said that sometimes the "tripper to Harpur Hill leaves before the Fly and sometimes after it!"

Both the Station Master and his 14 year old son were 'busy at breakfast' whilst unknowingly the other participants were setting the stage for this unfortunate affair.

THE TRAIN STAFF

Exploration of the handling of the Train Staff reveals an amazing state of affairs, as there appears to have been no conformity between the men as to how this "lump of wood" inscribed "L to HH" was to be used, or even who was responsible for issuing it, or it's safe-keeping! Station Master James Wardle was the senior person in charge, as well as being the Goods Agent etc; he states that Driver Chappell should either have got the staff, or seen it, which is, by my (JMB's) training in these matters quite correct, but Wardle says that there was no rule which said that the Train Staff should be deposited with him to ensure its security and maintain the integrity of the (so called) traffic control system. Yet, he also says that he would have reported any driver who left the station without permission. How did he expect drivers to get access to the Train Staff, or permission to depart if he was "busy at breakfast?"

My (JMB's) belief is that possession or otherwise of the "Train Staff" had very little to with train working at all on that section of the High Peak railway. Fireman Goodwin had to 'fetch it' off Lupton's engine that morning; as we know Lupton worked the Harpur Hill section up to the previous day, so it would not have taken much of an oversight for that Train Staff to have finished up at Bunsall on Lupton's engine, and you can 'bet your bottom dollar' that it did exactly this on occasions. This Train Staff was not of the type (for instance with an Annettes Key on the end) which gave access via ground frames into sidings, as the later ones did, it was to all practical purposes just a 'lump of wood' which the Line Manager and Locomotive Inspector at Cromford (Note their absence from the enquiry) had issued, along with some very lax and suspect instructions.

To summarise what the men said regarding the 'Train Staff."
Driver Goodwin stated: "he always had it on the loco."
Driver Chappell stated: "he went with it more often than without it!"
Station Master Wardle stated: "it had to be taken or seen."
Guard Melbourne stated: "Chappell had no right to go without it."
So what conclusions are we to draw? The two drivers are obviously not being entirely frank, or so it would appear from their statements, indeed how could they be, for if Goodwin followed Chappell every day, only one of them could have been in possession of the "Train Staff" unless there were two!!

The Inspecting Officer stated that full instructions for the daily use of the Train Staff were printed at the bottom of the April 1874 time-table; he also noted that the L&NWR management did not bother to do the same at the bottom of the October 1875 issue;

perhaps there were now too many trips to be able to plan the use of the Train Staff precisely, so, instead of introducing Staff and Ticket working, they left it to the men on the ground to sort out on an 'ad hoc' basis.

The result of this official acceptance of the sloppy working more or less forced upon the men of the High Peak railway, led to the untimely death of a completely innocent party, Fireman George Tumington, with the blame being apportioned to Driver Chappell, and the L&NWR having its knuckles rapped for allowing such loose working. Instructions for the safe operation of the line, including Staff and Ticket Working were soon in place.

We are fortunate enough to have a photograph (page 42) of Driver Chappell in later days, when he is seen with a Webb 17" coal engine at Buxton not long before his retirement.

William Chappell was not of British origin, having left Germany he came to this country in the mid 1800's with his three brothers, each of them settling in a different county. William, obviously worked at the southern end of the High Peak district, migrating towards Ladmanlow when steam locomotives took over from horses, and, we learn, had been a driver for some seventeen years before the accident occurred. Driver Chappell moved to Buxton L&NWR depot in June 1892, along with the rest of the High Peak men on the closure of Ladmanlow Depot. His grandson was a guard at Buxton, and his two great-grandsons became drivers, Dennis Plant at Rowsley, and Eric Plant who has loaned to us the photograph of his great-grandfather at Buxton.

A major problem must have been clearing of the line, and bringing in extra locomotives to cover for those involved in the crash. Chappell's engine No 1835 was broken up in January 1876, doubtless beyond repair, Goodwin's loco survived 'to fight again.' What a problem the Longsight brake-down crews must have had; all their equipment including at least one Crewe goods 2-4-0 loco had to be hauled up Shallcross and Bunsall inclines, no doubt the Southern end of the High Peak could muster up one spare loco to assist with traffic, at that end, probably C&HPR No 6 (by then LNWR 1945.) The weather would also heighten their problems, and trying to clear up the debris with 10 ton hand cranes would be a lengthy process, not to mention the removal of the wrecked locomotives, back to Longsight, all in all a very difficult task during which the normal traffic on the line would be at a standstill, ironically it was the extra run worked by Driver Goodwin intending to obviate delays to the LIME TRAFFIC that initiated this most unfortunate and tragic accident.

NEW RULES AND REGULATIONS APRIL 1891

That the London & North Western Railway Co., took the criticisms to heart is confirmed by reference to a document that G.E.Mawby, District Superintendent issued from his Manchester Office in April, 1891. Headed LONDON AND NORTH WESTERN RAILWAY, RULES AND REGULATIONS APPLYING TO THE CROMFORD AND HIGH PEAK SECTION, The preamble ran "The following Special Rules and Regulations must be observed by all Servants engaged on the Cromford and High Peak Section, in addition to those contained in the General Book of Rules and Regulations. The fifteen pages of type-written instructions were formulated to embrace and obviate - it seems- the sort of situations that led to the 'Driver Chappell' collision.

Item 2. specified the nine sections of line, their working regulated by the relevant Train Staffs, and spelt out the Driver's responsibilities in this connection. Item No 3 was specific on the point that "No Train or Engine may enter any Section unless the Engine - Driver is in possession of the Train Staff belonging to that section, precise instructions then follow, but the principle of operation is clearly laid down. The physical aspect of the Train Staff for each section is described.

Much attention has been paid to 'trip workings.' Of particular interest is the Time-Table dealing with "Bunsall and Hurdlow - Alternate Weekly Working, and No.4. which has been designated '6.30am Whaley Bridge to Cromford. "Engine changes at Ladmanlow and Hurdlow. Engine from Ladmanlow takes Staff from Hurdlow (Top) to Hurdlow (Bottom) and returns from Hurdlow (Bottom) to Hurdlow (Top) assisting the 6.20am from Cromford.

Working No.16, 11.40am Shallcross to Cromford is annotated "Engine changes at Ladmanlow and again at Hurdlow, and Engine from Ladmanlow to Hurdlow runs No.17 "C" trip when required, that being Hurdlow Top 3.07pm to Hurdlow Bottom 3.14pm.

Other sections appearing in the District Superintendent's list of Rules and Regulations specifically cover the type of situation that gave rise to the 1875 collision e.g.

Supply of Empty Waggons

The Breaks-men working the 11.30am Cromford to Shallcross must obtain information from all the Stations of the number of empty Waggons required and communicate it to the Foreman on duty at Shallcross, who must order up the supply the same day." and even more pertinent:" Regulating Supply of Midland Empty Waggons to Load Limestone at Hopton, Middlewood, and other Quarries.

It will be the duty of the Locomotive Fireman-Breaks-man working between Cromford and High Peak Junction to inform the Clerk in charge at the Agent's Office, Cromford, the number of Midland Co's empty waggons on hand each morning, and the Clerk will telephone the information to the Loco .Engineman at Sheep pasture (Top of) and Middleton (Top of) to enable them to regulate the distribution of the empties to the various work. THE BREAKS-MEN FROM HURDLOW TO FURNISH SIMILAR INFORMATION AS REGARDS THE NUMBER OF EMPTY WAGONS WORKED TO HOPTON BY THEIR TRAINS."

To conclude this brief survey of a very comprehensive set of Working Instructions :

Shunting at Harpur Hill

"A Platelayer is appointed as Flagman to meet the trains and to protect them during the shunting of the Limited Kiln Sidings, and the Old Kiln Sidings each morning, and the following instructions must be carried out: No 1. Weekly Working. On arrival at Harpur Hill of the 5.40am. train Ladmanlow to Briggs' Siding, the flagman must take charge of Train Staff No 7... etc.etc.

If the 6.30am train, Briggs' Siding to Ladmanlow, be in sufficient time, it will be attached at the Old Kiln Sidings Junction to the 7.10am train, Harpur Hill to Bunsall, and the two trains will run together to Ladmanlow. The flagman will under these circumstances give Train Staff No 7 to the driver of the 7.10am train, Harpur Hill to Bunsall. If the 6.30am train Briggs' Siding to Ladmanlow be late, the flagman must allow the 7.10am train, Harpur Hill to Bunsall to go forward, in accordance with Rule 194."

A STAGE COACH ON RAILS

We have observed that when Wheatcroft's (page 10) obtained their licence to operate a passenger coach on the line between Cromford and Whaley, the C&HPR did not have the legal powers to run its own passenger trains, but obtained such authorization in the Parliamentary Act of 1855. Wheatcroft's also operated a stage-coach between Whaley Bridge and Manchester. An account in the Derby Mercury for 20 September 1854 of a journey over the C&HPR relates that the train consisted of one passenger carriage, with seats for 14 passengers 'inside' and sixteen 'outside'. It was drawn by one horse 'over all levels', the animal was changed at designated stations, and the passengers who remained in the carriages throughout learnt that ..."by adding two powerful 'breaks' to the carriage, all danger is avoided, for the conductor told us that he could stop the carriage on the steepest part of these inclines, by his 'breaks' in about one minute – consequently no one could feel the slightest fear."

Dr J. R. Hollick also recorded this account of passenger travel under the heading "Reminiscences of people who used the High Peak Passenger Trains:"

"Till about 1898 circa the opening of the Parsley Hay-Ashbourne line, a passenger coach was run at the end of goods trains. This open vehicle was of the cattle-truck style, and had boards for seats. Owing to the infrequency of the service one was apparently lucky if one got a train back the same day. The reason for the withdrawal of the passenger coach was the great number of accidents, passengers frequently being killed. (The Minninglow rag and bone seller being one of the last). Tickets were issued by the guard. Passengers

had to walk down the two 'inclined planes' (of which one was Hopton and the other presumably Middleton) the train not being run beyond Middleton bottom for passengers.'

A very old photograph depicts a brake 3rd of prehistoric design at the end of a goods train. This C&HPR passenger service was never mentioned in 'Bradshaw' but a service to Buxton over the 'High Peak Railway' operated by 'one engine in steam' is mentioned in an 1857 'Directory of Derbyshire'.

Fare Structure -Passenger Loadings. The 'restructuring' Act which received the Royal assent on 26 June 1855, empowered the Cromford & High Peak Railway to become carriers, and levy charges for passengers at the rate of 2d per mile, first class, 1½d per mile second class and 1d per mile third class, and authorised them to charge for the use of the Company's carriages at the rate of 1d, 1/2d and 1/4d per mile for access to the three classes respectively.

In the event, that contribution to income accruing from passenger traffic was negligible; during the first half of 1856, 383 passengers were carried in 10 passenger trains, the distance travelled was 500 miles, receipts £24; in the second half of the year (which included the summer season) 1,019 persons travelled in 150 passenger trains, the distance was 3,825 miles and the value of receipts £66 e.g. £90 for the year. In 1857 the number of passengers was 716, and the receipts £53, there was a very slight increase in 1858 to 820 carried and receipts £63, but in 1861 only 121 passengers had turned up and the receipts were £8: at this point the C&HPR was, leased to the L&NWR.

Ladmanlow Yard

Ladmanlow. 29 April 1955: The High Peak line between Ladmanlow Yard and Colliery Junction crossed the A54 Buxton to Macclesfield road by means of this narrow wrought-iron plate girder through span bridge which had been renewed in 1865, but the structure being a hazard to usurping road traffic was removed in 1958 when the track was lifted northwards towards Ladmanlow which in its day was one of the principal stations on the Cromford & High Peak Railway.

Harry Townley

Ladmanlow Yard. c.1935: Dr Hollick has walked in a northerly direction through and beyond the yard at Ladmanlow and then turned to take this panoramic style picture looking towards the Leek Road crossing; the typical L&NWR style signal post carrying two arms, one for each opposing direction, stands out very clearly and one must admire the hardiness of the High Peak railwaymen who kept the traffic moving whatever the weather conditions on such bleak and windswept expanses of the High Peak.

Dr.J.R.Hollick

Ladmanlow Yard, 1948: An unidentified 3F 0-6-0 locomotive departs in the direction of Colliery Junction depicted on previous pages, to pick up a 'raft' of empty wagons to be run around and placed on the Grin Branch for loading. After the closure of this line the storage of wagons was its final use; then as the track was lifted at Ladmanlow the unwanted wagons were moved for storage closer to Harpur Hill.

L.M.Hobdey

Ladmanlow Yard. 29 April 1955: Although awaiting track removal and demolition of the redundant buildings, the whole lay-out appears to be in remarkably good condition, with no hint of vandalism as would regrettably occur today. Five decades ago clearance of a site could be long delayed after the official date of abandonment. The engine shed which had been removed soon after closure of the line to Whaley Bridge and transfer of engines and men to Buxton stood just beyond the water tower. The cast-iron notice board appearing over the wall to the right of the gate reads "LONDON NORTH WESTERN RAILWAY - BEWARE OF THE TRAINS - LOOK BOTH UP AND DOWN THE LINE BEFORE YOU CROSS".

Harry Townley

Ladmanlow. 25 April 1953: North London tanks Nos **58856** and **58860** hauled the joint SLS/Manchester Locomotive Society train of four open trucks and three brake vans from Middleton Top to Friden, where 3F 0-6-0 No **43618** plus three corridor coaches took over and conveyed the party on to Ladmanlow where they were met by two cars carrying photographers and then the party was returned back to Hindlow and Buxton.

Harry Townley

Over the years at Ladmanlow

Ladmanlow. 25 April 1953: The lonely cottages of Grin Row are seen left, and whilst visitors on a joint tour by members of the Stephenson Locomotive Society and Manchester Locomotive Society look round the yard, their 'special' the loco carrying the reporting number W574 waits, with Warrington (8B) 3F 0-6-0 **43618** blowing off. The water tank is to the right of the yard and the level crossing gates beyond are open to road traffic. **Dr.J.R.Hollick**

Ladmanlow Yard. c.1890: Two locomotives were allocated to Ladmanlow depot, Crewe Goods 2-4-0's of both tank and tender types; depicted is No **3074** with Driver Townley. This locomotive began life in October 1854 as LNWR No **18** bearing the name of *Cerebus* the three-headed dog said by the Greeks to guard the entrance to Hades. (Burbage Tunnel!!) *Cerebus* was renumbered 17 in January 1857 and still in heroic mode renamed *Caliban.* The engine was then rebuilt in 1872 when its name was removed; in October 1879 it was placed on the duplicate list which for many old locomotives meant that they were close to being broken up, but not this one! It survived to be renumbered yet again on February 1887 as No **3074**, a number it carried until withdrawn from Buxton Depot in June 1897. Despite their frail appearance these engines were the motive power for the Middleton Top to Bunsall Top section from the 1860's to their end in 1897, the tank engine versions lasted slightly longer. No 3074 would do the Bunsall Top to Hopton Top run daily, its light build and flexible wheel-base allowing easy negotiation of Gotham Curve; the tender weather-board would have been of little protection on the wild Axe Edge. The Crewe Goods type locos had only axle-driven water pumps so at night the rails inside the shed were greased and with one engine leaning on the other the regulator would be opened whilst the boiler was filled as the wheels slipped. Fireman Oldfield, a young relief from Buxton was crushed between a loco and the shed door frame at Ladmanlow when the operation went wrong one night, but recovered to take the Foreman cleaners job at Buxton, a job which he held until his retirement. **J.M.Bentley collection**

A LOCOMOTIVE MISCELLANY

THE FIRST STEAM ENGINES ON THE C&HPR

Ladmanlow c 1890. Crewe Goods 2.4.0 tank No 3097, with Driver Townley, pose in the sunshine in Ladmanlow yard. 3097, one of the few members of the class to receive a cab, which must have offered just a little more protection for the crews than the rest of the cab-less variety, much needed in this very bleak location. This Crewe veteran was another with a fascinating history, starting life as a 2.4.0 tender locomotive No 295 *Penmaenmawr* in November 1852. August 1857 saw this and others transferred to the Lancaster & Carlisle Rly, becoming their No 58, only to be returned to the Crewe fold in August 1859 and numbered 521. In July 1870 rebuilding to a tank locomotive took place and in April 1883, No 521 became No 1875 in the company's duplicate list. Not the end of the story yet, for in November 1887, from a further duplicate list, the locomotive was allotted the number 3097, which it carried until withdrawal from Buxton depot in January 1903. Furthermore, the tale took another twist, as 3097 was sold to Fenton Colliery, Alsager, where she was still intact in 1914.

J.M.Bentley Collection

Railway historians have often debated the actual date when steam locomotives were first used on the C&HPR, and the following extracts from the late Dr J. R. Hollick's "High Peak Note-Book' are very relevant to the discussion.

"Messrs Robert Stephenson & Co., of Newcastle-upon-Tyne supplied locomotive No 45, appropriately named Peak in 1833 thought to have worked between Middleton Top to Hopton Bottom inclines. According to S. S. Scott, Mr E. Bury supplied No 22 and No 23 named *Liverpool* and *Bury* respectively in 1835. These were four-wheeled 'singles' of the classic Bury bar-frame design, with 12" x 18" inside cylinders. Presumably these became C&HPR No 2 and No 3. No 3 was apparently in existence (if not in service) in 1860 and 1861, since in both years the C&HPR gave their stock of engines as seven, but no further return was made owing to their arrangement with the LNWR.

A report in the "Derby Mercury" of 3rd February 1841, reproduced in part in the "Railway Times" three days later, said that a steam locomotive had undergone trials on the Cromford & High Peak Railway "a fortnight since" and that it was intended to construct two more engines. The locomotive was said to have had 'cylinders outside the framing and on a level with the centre of the wheels and the construction to be of "extreme simplicity". Designed by a Mr Leonard, the engine weighed about 5 tons 15 cwt and was said to cost 'a little more' than £400. It appears that this engine, dating from 1840, may have been altered about 1859 from an 0-4-0 tender to an 0-6-0 tank to become C&HPR No 4 so it might be assumed that No 5 could be a rebuild of a second 0-4-0, perhaps by Tayleur & Co., of the Vulcan Foundry, Makers No 175 of 1842, a six-coupled tender engine with 5 ft wheels and 14 in x 20 in cylinders. which was reputedly built for the C&HPR. The Daily Mercury's (3 Feb 1841) correspondent stated that 'the engine was in use throughout the week' 25th to 30th January 1841 and that he travelled with a steam train on 27th January, so locomotive working definitely appears to have commenced towards the end of January 1841.Would this would explain the mystery of how the C&HPR could 'build' two new engines in 1859-60? it also indicates that they may have had four or five engines in the 1840's and 1850's."

Systematic locomotive working would appear to have begun, states Dr Hollick, in 1855, with No 2, of the 2-2-0 type, with 3 ft leading wheels, and 4 ft 8 in driving wheels, 12 in x 18 in cylinders, built by Bury, Curtis & Kennedy, but this must have been obtained second-hand as Bury, Curtis

had ceased building engines by that date. These wheels were smaller than those usually fitted to Bury engines, so may have been specially supplied for work on the C&HPR, perhaps obtained from the Southern Division of the L&NWR. Although the High Peak line was leased to the L&NWR on 30 June, 1862, the locomotives were not taken into stock until 1871. Then, engine No 2, became No 2039 and later duplicate No 1942; it was then lettered 'B' and used as a stationary engine, until scrapped in 1882. Four other C&HPR engines taken over were 0-6-0T engines Nos 3, 5, 6, and 7, the first two possibly acquired second-hand by the High Peak line before the arrival of the L&NWR; they had 3 ft wheels and 10 in x 12 in cylinders. No.s. 6 and 7 Works Nos 435 and 436 of 1860, were Vulcan Foundry engines, saddle tanks with o/s cylinders 9 in x 15 in. 17 ft 0¾ ins long and 9 ft 10½ in high, 3 ft wheels on a wheelbase 8 ft 6 ins, working pressure 100 lbs psi. One engine worked between Hindlow and Ladmanlow and the other between Hindlow and Hopton.

No 4 became LNWR No 2040 later No 1943, and in March 1877 was transferred to the LNWR Locomotive Machinery Department and as such carried the designation "D" on the side-sheet of the open footplate. It was scrapped at Crewe on 23rd May 1882. In 1878 when the LNWR line from Llandudno Junction to Blaenau Ffestiniog was under construction the rebuilt No 4 turned up at Dolwyddelen, on works trains as reported by the late Max Dunn. In any case, the operation of any steam locomotive on the C&HPR was greatly disadvantaged by the state of the track, which still comprised the rudimentary cast-iron edge rails, that had long been replaced by those of wrought iron on other railways, These brittle C&HPR rails broke under the weight of steam engines, furthermore because horses were used for haulage, the old fashioned stone blocks on which the cast iron rails were laid could not readily be replaced by wooden cross-sleepers. When the L&NW Rly, took over the working of the High Peak line in April 1861, they drafted in a varied assortment of motive power, to supplement the miscellaneous array of C&HPR locomotives, five of which did duty until their withdrawal in 1871. Further reference will later be made to the involved story of C&HPR locomotive engines, and in the decade following the amalgamation, at one time or another High Peak metals were host to former Birkenhead Railway 2-2-2 tender engines, a 2-4-0 side tank, and 0-4-0T formerly on the Kendal & Windermere Railway, also the 0-4-0 well tank built by George England & Co., in 1857 for the Sandy & Potton Railway, that became the Wantage Tramroad's famous Shannon. Engines that had formerly worked on the St Helens Railway, and Cockermouth & Workington Railway, also put in an appearance.

The Grin Branch
- another
High Peak Junction

Grin Branch signal post. c.1950: In responding to the indications of this Grin Branch Junction signal post, the lower arm was obeyed by Buxton Lime Co., engines going in and out of the Branch. The other arm controlled movements by trains from the direction of Hindlow. It was dismantled 7 June 1950. *Harry Townley*

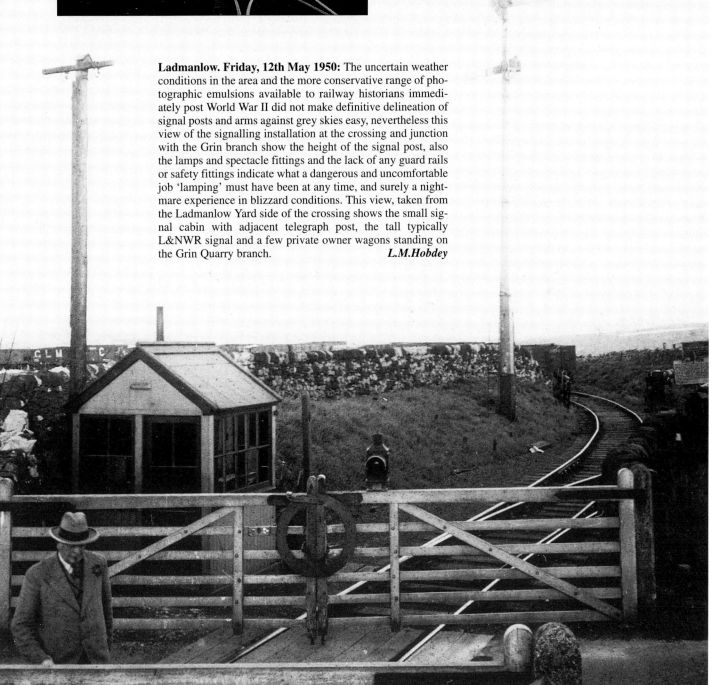

Ladmanlow. Friday, 12th May 1950: The uncertain weather conditions in the area and the more conservative range of photographic emulsions available to railway historians immediately post World War II did not make definitive delineation of signal posts and arms against grey skies easy, nevertheless this view of the signalling installation at the crossing and junction with the Grin branch show the height of the signal post, also the lamps and spectacle fittings and the lack of any guard rails or safety fittings indicate what a dangerous and uncomfortable job 'lamping' must have been at any time, and surely a nightmare experience in blizzard conditions. This view, taken from the Ladmanlow Yard side of the crossing shows the small signal cabin with adjacent telegraph post, the tall typically L&NWR signal and a few private owner wagons standing on the Grin Quarry branch. *L.M.Hobdey*

Ladmanlow.c.1900: 0-6-0 DX goods engine No **3393** is seen sometime between March 1899 and January 1901. Originally No 543 built in June 1869 not destined to be rebuilt as a Special DX with vacuum brake, Webb boiler etc., put on the duplicate list in March 1899 and cut up in January 1901. Note, only a hand operated tender brake is fitted, firemen soon developed strong arms operating these whilst shunting, an operation known as "working the treadmill" and carried out hundreds of times in each day's work, in addition to all the other tasks the poor fireman had to do. The trip down the 1 in 41 gradient from Harpur Hill to Hindlow must have seen much back-gear work on these engines.

J.M.Bentley collection

Ladmanlow. 12 May 1950: A general view of Grin Row cottages with three wagons standing on the Grin Quarry Branch, the kilns are just visible (left) as is the double signal controlling the High Peak line. In the early days the indications of the large arms were obeyed by High Peak drivers while a small arm controlled movements by the quarry's engine drivers. The quarry company had running powers over High Peak metals to Ladmanlow Colliery Junction when carrying coal to the quarry's kilns; there were also B.L.F. engines from Old Harpur and at the time when Dr Hollick, his friends and associates explored the railway this now desolate area was a hive of activity.

Harry Townley

Ladmanlow 29 April 1955: This lonely level crossing and junction with the Grin Branch had a peculiar fascination for both historians of the line and its photographers and this very definitive picture of the site includes the stop and await instruction signs extreme left and off centre that guarded both lines, that on the left erected on a small platform cut into the low cutting, both signs capable of being illuminated when required. Across the road in the yard behind the gates is the wooden Ladmanlow Goods Shed, whilst the guardian cottage appears above the dry-stone wall so typical of the terrain of the High Peak line.

Harry Townley

The Grin Branch

Ladmanlow c.1948: One of Buxton's ubiquitous 3F 0-6-0's moves away from the lonely hamlet of Ladmanlow, with its isolated cottages where the inhabitants were literally marooned for periods during the severe winters experienced five decades ago. The unidentified 3F and its crew have just completed shunting work; loads of lime in sheeted wagons and limestone from the Grin Quarry are next to the locomotive, and Driver Arthur Robinson (Senior) looks back from the cab towards the photographer, who was doubtless well known to him from many previous visits.   *L.M.Hobdey*

Grin Quarry Branch: L&NW 0-4-0ST No **3003** on loan to the company whilst its own loco was under repair.   *J.M.Bentley collection*

Grin Branch. C.1935: The Quarry Cos Andrew Barclay 0-6-0ST *Clyde* just clear of the High Peak Line. LMS man in charge of movements posing for photographer.   *Dr.J.R.Hollick*

(Right) Clay Cross Company's Grin Branch. nd: The firm's vertical boilered Sentinel 0-4-0 loco pauses across the Ladmanlow to Harpur Hill road for photos, the crew unconcerned about blocking the highway.

Dr.J.R.Hollick

(Below) Grin Branch c.1948: Looking towards the junction with the High Peak line, with wooden bodied wagons on display and a distant motor car climbing the A54 road over Axe Edge.

L.M.Hobdey

Ladmanlow 12 May 1950: Another view of the signalling, the crossing and junction with the Grin Branch. Despite being a 'goods only' station, Ladmanlow qualified for a Station Master, the last to hold the post being Ralph Tomlinson.

Harry Townley

THE ROUTE *DESCRIBED*

On emerging from Burbage Tunnel, Buxton would be sighted far below and if 'right time' had been kept, the train would come to a stand at Ladmanlow" at 8.15am; it had taken 1 hr 5 min to cover the 7 miles from Whaley Bridge.

The stations on the High Peak line were then, in the 1880's mostly without name boards and the buildings stated to be "little more than sheds," their locations "off the beaten track." The train would be shunted' at Ladmanlow, wagons being removed or added as required and **The Fly**, in the guise of Train No 6 was then booked to depart at 8.30am. The route continued, past Diamond Hill, and the 'stony' slopes of Solomon's Temple, to Harpur Hill, which would be reached at 8.45am.

Stanley Moor

Stanley Moor, 25 April 1963: A 3F 0-6-0 No **43618** in the distance is negotiating the old L&NWR deviation of 1875 near the Stanley Moor Reservoir, this was the site of the 17 December 1875 head-on collision when one fireman was killed. The original line passed round the back of the hill on the right, the deviation joining the original line a little ahead of the point where the locomotive is seen in this picture. The area around this hill was the setting of a murder story by Burbage born writer John Buxton Hilton concerning a dubious character Thos. Beresford, a C&HPR driver and an imaginary village called Piper's Fold. The description of Driver Beresford and his fireman Jack Plant fits the line wonderfully, an inventory of poaching tackle carried on the engine, stopping to set traps and retrieve the catches was not altogether unknown in the 'good old days' of the line.   *Harry Townley*

L&NWR High Peak line deviation. c.1932: The first picture taken by Dr Jack Hollick early in his explorations of the High Peak Line, shows the Safety & Mines Research buildings in the background; that bodies 'explosion tunnel' for experimental purposes was built on the former track bed of the original High Peak line, which the deviation in the right foreground rendered redundant.   *Dr.J.R.Hollick*

Buxton: This is a photograph of Driver Chappell who was involved in the 1875 accident referred to previously, but in happier times on the footplate of a 17" Webb 'coal engine' not long before his retirement. An experienced long service driver before the Turncliffe accident occurred, when the L&NWR Ladmanlow Depot was closed in 1892, Driver Chappell moved to the Buxton Depot with the rest of the men.

Photo courtesy Eric Plant

L&NWR High Peak line deviation. 26 October 1965: A melancholy sight and duty for 4F No **44271** featured here was to remove the last lot of stored wagons from this section, of the railway, the redundant vehicles coupled in a sorry procession to No 44271 leave High Peak metals for the last time to be scrapped. Soon after this dismal task, which all concerned knew was the beginning of the end of an era, was completed, the track was removed.

J.M.Bentley

Old Harpur. c.1963: This is a close-up view of the cutting and bridge just visible through the gloom in the rear of No **44059's** tender in the photograph (right). It was taken whilst No 44059 was placing its van in the RAF sidings. Even now, although the area has been absorbed into the Harpur Hill Industrial Estate the historic bridge still survives.

J.M.Bentley

Old Harpur. c.1963: Former LMS 4F 0-6-0 No **44059** of a class introduced in 1924 based on a Midland design, but with reduced boiler mountings, has placed a single van for the RAF sidings in position and is about to draw its brake-van back out onto the 'main line' prior to propelling back to Hindlow before working traffic from Briggs or Hindlow to Buxton.

J.M.Bentley

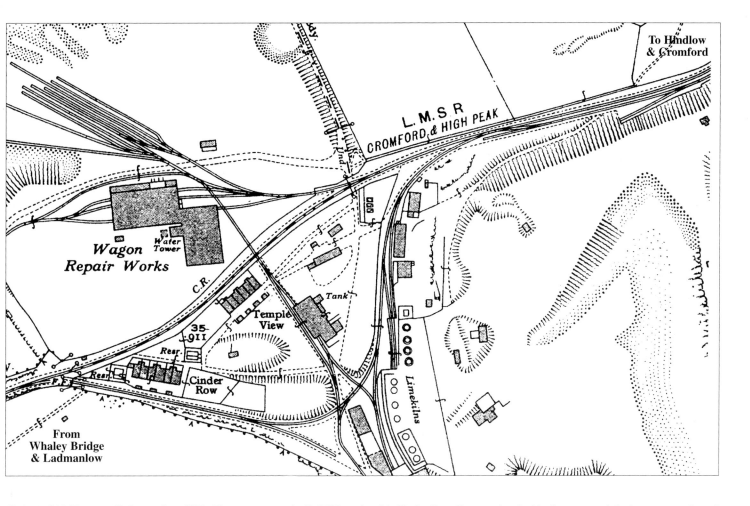

From
**Whaley Bridge
& Ladmanlow**

**Wagon
Repair Works**

Water
Tower

C.R.

35
911

Resr.

Resr.

F.E.

**Temple
View**

Tank

**Cinder
Row**

Limekilns

L.M.S.R
CROMFORD & HIGH PEAK

To Hindlow
& Cromford

(Below) Old Harpur, 10 September 1950. The entrance to the RAF Tunnels with Cinder Row Cottages just inside the gates and the huge excavation of the Imperial Chemical Industries Quarry towering above them.
E.R.Morten

(Above) **Old Harpur. 10 September 1950:** This location with Temple View cottages prominent adjacent to the railway is facing north, just beyond the 90 degree crossing where the 4F 0-6-0 locomotive and van are featured in scenes following. The edge of the ICI Quarry appears top right.

E.R.Morten

Harpur Hill

Old Harpur. Early 1960's: These three views (above, left and below) of the 90 degree crossing at the ICI Wagon shops at Old Harpur. This type of crossing was not common on our railway system; with no adjacent signal box a movement over this crossing required proper arrangements between private owner and railway company shunter, under whose supervision the line was worked. 4F 0-6-0 No **44364** is propelling a brake-van back towards Harpur Hill and No **44271** on 8 Nov 1965 heading towards the Mines Research sidings to pick up a van, the igloo, right is a ICI 'blasting' protective shelter.

J.M.Bentley

Harpur Hill

The terrain was now wild and bleak, with the only signs of life, a hare starting from the line side, "clucking" grouse and foraging crows, rising before the train at the last minute, as the **'Fly'** rattled and gyrated on its way. Arrival at Hindlow (12·5 miles) was booked for 9.00am.

(Right) Old Harpur. Sept 1950: On this occasion the photographer has his back to the 90 degree crossing. The points to the left are approximately on the original line of the early Cromford & High Peak Railway, which was replaced by the line in the right foreground, the old line becoming part of the BLF Wagon Works complex. The photograph on Page 46 featuring 4F 0-6-0 No **44083** and 2-8-0 No **48275** was taken from a position beside the telegraph pole just left of centre where the line of wagons is standing in this scene.   *E.R.Morten*

Fireman Ron Bretherton looks out of **43296's** cab towards the photographer, on the left of the locomotive Harpur Hill Road can be seen and in the background on the right of the picture the new RAF houses were being built.   *E.R.Morten*

Old Harpur, 11 June 1963: A 'clear-out' of stored wagons needed the services of both the 7.30am and 7.40am Hindlow engines. The 4F, No **44083** eases around the grass covered sidings, whilst 8F No **48275** awaits instructions on the main line.
J.M.Bentley

Buxton 3F 0-6-0 No 43296 shunts at Old Harpur about ten years before the above picture was taken.
E.R.Morten

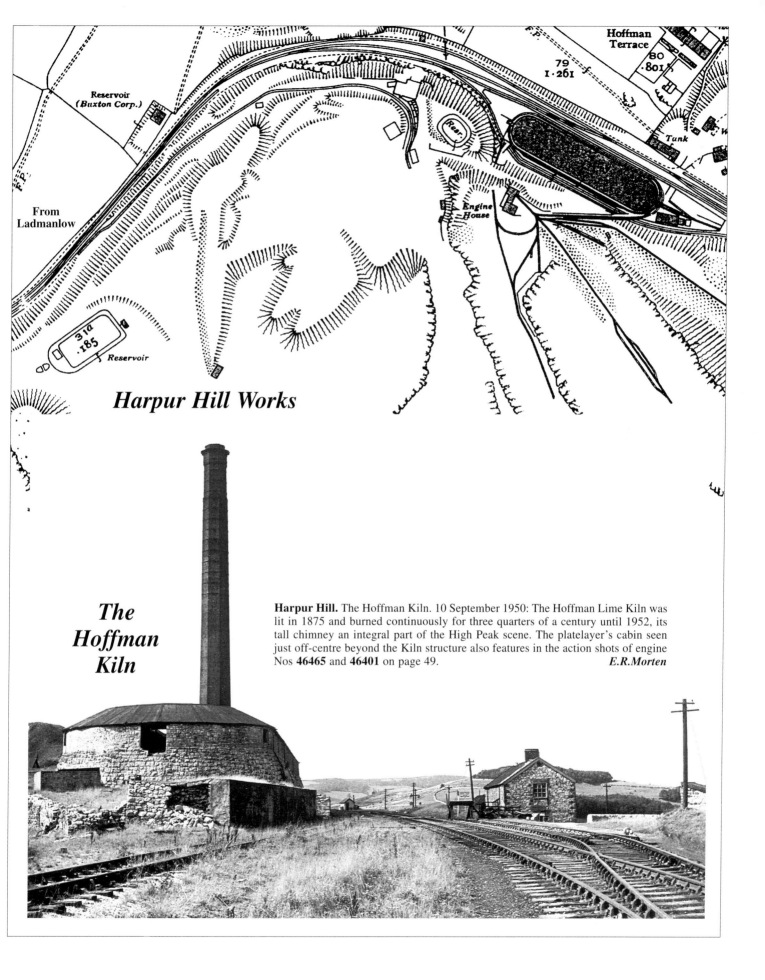

Harpur Hill Works

The Hoffman Kiln

Harpur Hill. The Hoffman Kiln. 10 September 1950: The Hoffman Lime Kiln was lit in 1875 and burned continuously for three quarters of a century until 1952, its tall chimney an integral part of the High Peak scene. The platelayer's cabin seen just off-centre beyond the Kiln structure also features in the action shots of engine Nos **46465** and **46401** on page 49.

E.R.Morten

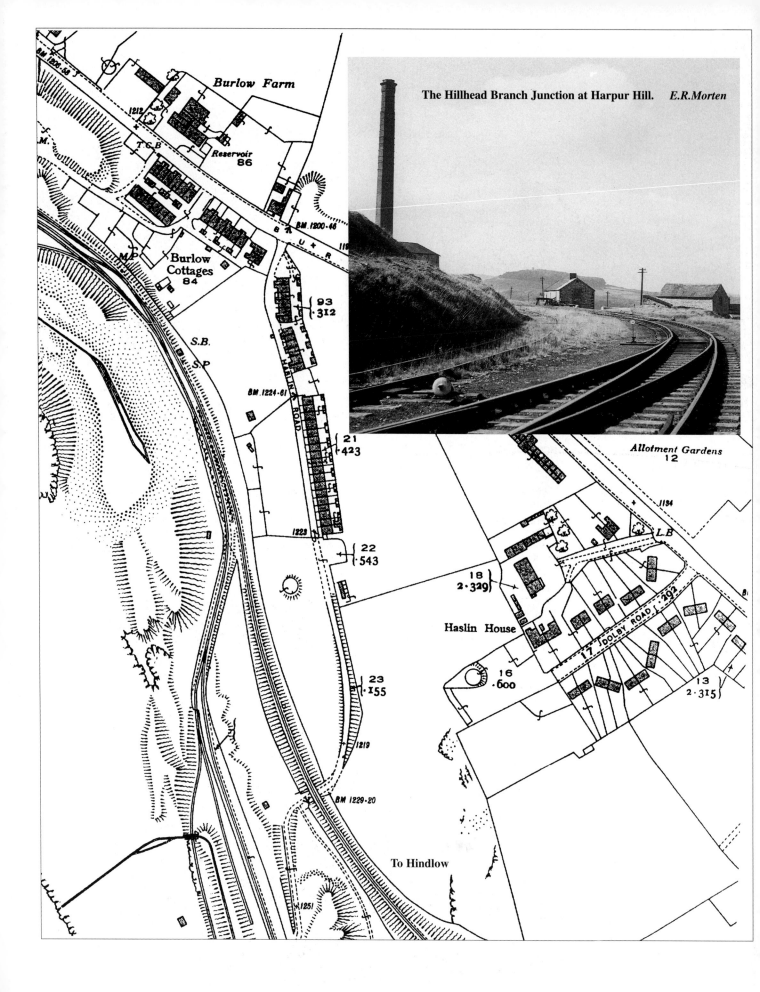

The Hillhead Branch Junction at Harpur Hill. *E.R.Morten*

Burlow Farm

Reservoir
86

Burlow
Cottages
84

To Hindlow

Allotment Gardens
12

L.B

Haslin House

DOLBY ROAD

(Above left) Old Harpur. 17 June 1963: A view of the line from the footplate of No **46465** as it heads towards Old Harpur; a bleak day in the Peak District. The black dots in the sky are not the photographer regrets indicative of ample bird life but the results of keeping one's camera permanently on a steam engine footplate.

(Above right) Harpur Hill. 3 March 1966: Beneath a spectacular moorland sky, as the engine's exhaust rises to mingle with the banks of cumulus cloud, Ivatt 2MT 2-6-0 No **46401** sets its train of 28 tippler wagons back towards Hill Head Sidings with Driver Ron Bretherton looking out from the cab. The ability of these small taper boiler engines with a tractive effort of 17,140 lb to lift 30 empties up the 1 in 41 gradient from Hindlow without assistance was quite outstanding. A good run at the bank, with a box full of fire, full second regulator, letting the wheel down to full lead gradually would, if rail conditions were good, just get the train to the summit at Harpur Hill. These tippler wagons transported stone from the Peak District to the sugar beet factories in the eastern counties of the country. A typical plate-layer's cabin sited on the left of the picture completes this nostalgic scene.

Both J.M.Bentley

Top of Harpur Bank.1953: Ex Midland 3F 0-6-0 No **43618** at the summit of the 1 in 41 from Hindlow with the gradient post on the left marking the transition from gradient to level. Carrying the reporting number W574, No 43618 is in charge of the Stephenson Locomotive Society/Manchester Locomotive Society 'HIGH PEAK RAIL TOUR' which proved so popular that another similar excursion was operated later in the same year.

Harry Townley

Hillhead Curve

Hillhead Curve. 27 February 1964: 4F 0-6-0 No **44497** is propelling its train slowly towards Hillhead Quarry Sidings; it has just 'hit-up' its brake-van which has gone sailing round the far bend and, with a bit of luck is now located at the rear of the loaded wagons all ready to be brought out. What fun was had by all when, as frequently happened, the hill mist fell and enveloped the area so that not a thing could be seen, then reliance had to be placed on the shunter's whistle to control movements, so the engine had to be worked as quietly as possible.

J.M.Bentley

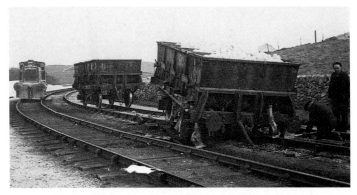

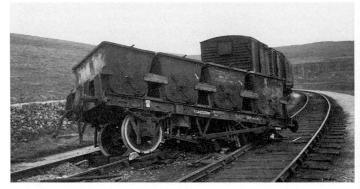

Hillhead Quarry Sidings, 25 April 1969: As mentioned in the previous caption, shunting during misty conditions could be troublesome, especially with 20-30 wagons attached as was in this case and a noisy class 25 diesel locomotive. The three blasts on the shunters whistle to stop have not been heard, resulting in the collision seen in the two photographs. The steam crane had to approach this accident with great care as the bend was just about the limit it could navigate.

photos S.Cameron

Hillhead Curve: A footplate view from 2MT No **46480** of a ballast train being propelled to Harpur Hill where the motive power for working the train forward would be waiting to take over from the 2MT 2-6-0.

J.M.Bentley

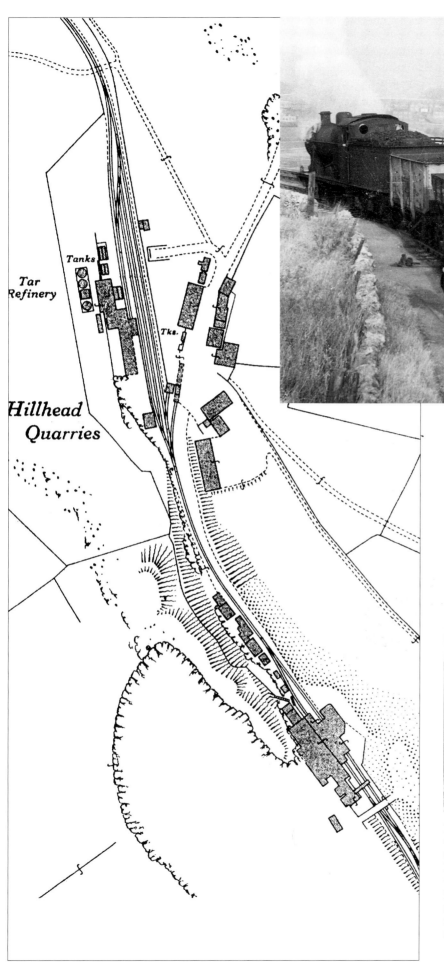

Hillhead Quarry

(Above) Hillhead Quarry Sidings. 8 November 1965: Just a few weeks away from its withdrawal (on 1 Jan 1966) Buxton depot's last 4F class locomotive No **44271** shunts at Hillhead Quarry Sidings. Shunter Bill Nadin walks, pole in hand, whilst Driver Albert Bowers follows his instructions. The two 21 ton hopper wagons stand on an adjacent road which was still laid with C&HPR stone-block sleepers when it was closed, the more modern bull-head chairs being fastened by bolts directly into the stone.

J.M.Bentley

Hillhead Quarry Yard. c.1964: Buxton based 4F 0-6-0 No **44059** stands on what had been the C&HPR main line, awaiting the shunter's permission to set back towards Harpur Hill; normally the loco would be facing the other way round, but with this being a right-hand drive engine, its driver, Albert Bowers preferred to be on his normal side for shunting purposes, however this meant a tender-first run up the 1 in 41 gradient from Hurdlow, which was not the easiest or most pleasant of things to do.

J.M.Bentley

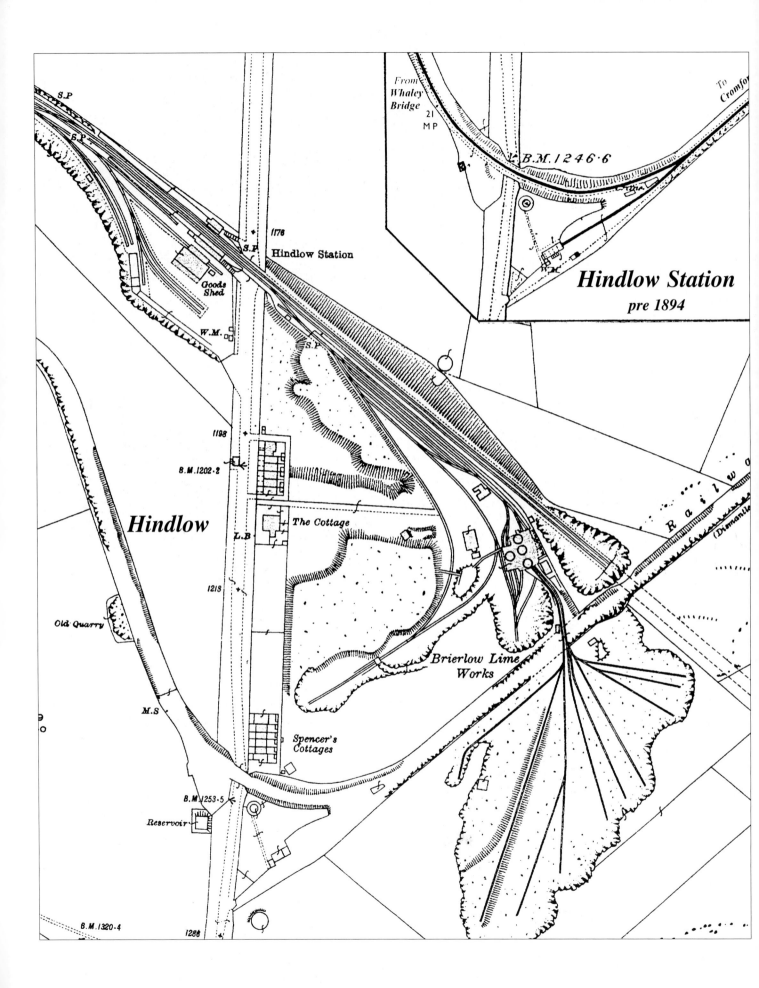

S.P

S.P

From
Whaley
Bridge

To
Cromfo

21
M.P

B.M.1246.6

Hindlow Station

Hindlow Station

pre 1894

1176

S.P

Hindlow Station

Goods
Shed

W.M.

S.P

1198

Railw

(Dismantle

B.M.1202.2

Hindlow

The Cottage

L.B

1218

Old Quarry

Brierlow Lime
Works

M.S

Spencer's
Cottages

B.M.1253.5

Reservoir

B.M.1320.4

1286

52

Hindlow

Hindlow Box 1 July 1962: This authentic L&NWR type 4 box had its frame extended to 37 levers in 1928, there was a 1 in 60 gradient past the box which was closed 30 June 1982. This location marked the southern end of the Buxton & High Peak Junction Railway No 2 line from Harpur Hill which came into being as a result of the abandonment of a section of the High Peak line between Ladmandlow and Shallcross. This line is the nearest of the three in view. **Don Rowland**

(Centre) Hindlow. n.d. An early view of the station looking south with the northern portal of Hindlow Tunnel in the distance. The lime works which were to develop to the right still had to make their mark and the recently abandoned section of the C&HP can be seen at a higher level running at right angles to the "new" line. The scene is pure L&NWR with the "Crewe hallmark" stamped all over the locomotive, station buildings, furnishings and fittings. **J.M.B Collection**

(Below) Hindlow. 25 April 1953: Just south of the station, with Beswick's Lime Works adjacent to the tunnel, a three coach 'special' carrying members of the joint SLS/Manchester Locomotive Society Rail Tour hurries by. This tour of the High Peak line was so popular that it was repeated on 27 June following. **Harry Townley**

(Above) **Hurdlow 1 July 1962:** The old route of the C&HPR lies across the hillside behind the station, between the points marked **A - B**. Brierlow farm is just beyond the sky line   *Don Rowland*

THE ROUTE *CONTINUED*

HINDLOW - Dowlow - HURDLOW (Incline No 5)

The line between Hindlow and Hurdlow, was constructed with a 1 in 16 incline, 850 yards in length, operated until 2 January 1869, its last day of working, after which it was abandoned and replaced by the Hurdlow Deviation, which had a maximum gradient of 1 in 60 and so could be worked by adhesion using ordinary locomotives. Train No 6 terminated at Hurdlow (Foot of) 16·5 miles reached at the booked time of 9.30am.

The guard, engine and crew were usually changed here, and water supplies for the area were conveyed in tanks from Ladmanlow. **The Fly** now assumed its final designation as Train No 7 departing at 9.35am.

The three photographs show the site of this triangle at closer range and that above left, depicts the line going off toward Brierlow Grange Farm, from which point it then made its way round Brierlow to Hindlow.

J.M.Bentley

Briggs Sidings

Briggs Sidings, 29 August 1964. Former LNER B1 4-6-0 No **61158** tops the five mile climb from Buxton with a Railway Correspondence & Travel Society special train. This picture shows the C&HPR track bed going off on the left of the train from the notice board entitled "FREIGHT TRAINS TO STOP AND PIN DOWN BRAKES." The C&HPR track led to the triangle, the site on the far left of the picture, then over the bridge and away to the right and around Brierlow. The purpose of this triangle is obscure, turning vans could have been one of its uses, as the first vans only had doors on one side. The locos on this section always ran chimney forwards to Whaley Bridge. *Harry Townley*

Briggs Sidings. Hindlow. Winter 1962: In this typical High Peak snow scene plough engine 0-8-0 No **49210** leading with 4F 0-6-0 No **44339** in the rear stand beside the signal box, opened in June 1894, and closed 18 May 1969 when the line to Buxton was singled. Fireman Peter Cook stands beside the engines and a member of the permanent way gang clears away snow from the points extreme left. *J.M.Bentley*

Briggs Siding. Late 1930's: The entrances to Messrs. Briggs' and Dowlow Sidings were on the right-hand side of our picture, in part obscured by 0-6-0 No **4549** and its lengthy retinue of assorted wagons, whilst the signal box opened in June 1894 is similarly out of sight to the left and behind the photographer. The box was closed on 18 May 1969 when the line from Buxton was singled.   *J.M.Bentley collection*

Dowlow. c.1890: One of the old tenders, converted to serve as water carriers which were such a feature of the C&HPR, was parked on this ramp at the top of the Hurdlow deviation to provide a supply point for locomotives. By this time the elderly 2-4-0 Crewe Goods engine (in 1887) had been renumbered as 3083 and survived for a further five years until withdrawn in 1892. From the huge pile of clinker behind the two standing figures it would appear that whilst engines were taking water the opportunity was also taken to clean the fire.   *J.M.Bentley collection*

Hurdlow Bank

Hurdlow Bank: Former Midland Railway 3F 0-6-0 No **43387** lifts the SLS/MLS special up the hill amongst the dry stone walls, so characteristic of the area, before the removal of the up line. The load of four bogie coaches would cause the 3F little trouble on the 1 in 60 gradient, but one wonders how C&HPR loco men of yore were taxed on this hill with an old Crewe goods 2-4-0 locomotive with its 120 lbs per sq in boiler pressure, but remembering that with the exception of the Hopton Incline no other gradients of any note faced the trains which were locomotive hauled.   *L.M.Hobdey*

Hurdlow Bank. 2 Sept 1964: 5MT 2-6-0 No **42941** stands in charge of a Permanent Way train of sleepers being unloaded by that department's staff. Over the years the surrounding fields provided a wondrous crop of mushrooms for train crews, who arrived back at the depot with all available containers, including hats, filled to the brim. A careful look-out for these delicacies would be made whilst descending the incline, and a stop would be made on the return journey to pick this rich harvest. It is interesting to look back at the way in which different drivers treated the descent of the 1 in 60 incline, especially with the ex L&NWR 0-8-0's some holding onto their trains until nearly at Hurdlow, others like Sam Bennett held the train back only for a short while, then 'letting it go.' *What a ride that was, tender first with a Super D,* especially when the sharp right-hand bend beyond Hurdlow station was taken as fast as the 4 ft 5 in driving wheels would allow!   *J.M.Bentley*

Top of Hurdlow: This view north from a point where the railway crossed the Hurdlow Town to Longnor road shows the old track bed in use as a farm track. The grounded van body rekindles thoughts of passing trains of well over a hundred years ago. A short distance beyond this point the farmland vanished into quarrying development. *G.K.Fox*

Above Hurdlow: The eastern face of the embankment seen in the picture below *G.K.Fox*

Hurdlow Incline(s)

One of the first sections to be abandoned in 1869 saw the removal of the highest working part of the High Peak Railway. The selection of photographs here highlight possibly the bleakest of locations on the line. Indeed, railway lines are known for generating trees and vegetation, but these scenes, recorded 130 years after the last train ran, illustrate how even mother nature baulks at such expansion in such inhospitable climatic conditions.

Above Hurdlow: From a higher vantage point a short distance from the level crossing the line continues with another reverse curve to take it near to the erstwhile Hurdlow Station. The 'township' of Hurdlow can be seen above the trees on the left of the picture. The occupation bridge (or cattle creep) has withstood a century of reduced maintenance. *G.K.Fox*

Top of Hurdlow: The abandoned railway bequeathed this fine stone faced embankment, so reminiscent of the Cromford & High Peak. Once again we see the difficulty facing vegetation in this remote region as the line curves yet again on its way south. *G.K.Fox*

Hurdlow Incline: The lower end of Hurdlow Incline is crossed by the same road as that mentioned previously. The electricity pylons have long marked the route of the erstwhile railway, a landmark which looks even more impressive from the nearby A515. *G.K.Fox*

High Peak Deviation

(Right) **Hurdlow Bank. 5 September 1964:** This being the C&HPR's own deviation that rendered the old Hurdlow Incline redundant, was doubled and re-aligned by the L&NWR, following the opening of the line from Buxton, but this nostalgic view from the footplate of 2MT 2-6-0 No **46401** as it climbs the bank towards Dowlow illustrates very clearly as the locomotive approaches the bridge, how the route was singled again when the rails of the Up line were lifted in 1959; ballast deposited in the 'four-foot' awaits the attention of members of the Permanent Way Department.

J.M.Bentley

(Below) **Hurdlow Incline (former site) September 1998:** In this open country it is not difficult, viewing these illustrations to picture how the original Hurdlow Incline, No 5, between Hopton and Bunsall, rising 160 feet in its 850 yard climb at a gradient of 1 in 16 would have looked prior to 1869, when it was abandoned by the C&HPR in favour of the new route from Briggs to Hurdlow bottom; the electricity poles observed in these scenes follow the route of the old line through to Dowlow. *G.K.Fox*

(Above)   **Hurdlow:** Dr Hollick believed this picture in his collection, taken on the Tuesday after Easter, 1929, to be of one of the special trains run for the Flagg Moor Steeplechases. In that case this would be one of four workings from the Buxton direction which arrived at Hurdlow to deposit the 'punters' between 11.54am and 12.30pm. The returning racegoers specials left Hurdlow between 4.25 and 5.55pm. The station was officially closed on 15 August 1949 but non-time tabled calls were made by service trains for the benefit of local railway employees or their families. The site of Hurdlow station is now the point where the High Peak Trail commences.

Dr.J.R.Hollick

(Centre) Hurdlow, 1963: Following removal of the Up Line, only station platforms at the closed Hurdlow station remain. This very clear view shows the section of abandoned C&HP route that was Hurdlow Incline, between the points marked **C - D.**

P.E.Baughan

Hurdlow Station c.1955: The quiet rusticity of the area four decades ago is evident in this picture of the station, taken across the road, the fencing in the foreground and raised cattle dock at the end of the platform are complementary to the more atypical dry-stone walling, whilst the whitewashed structure of the essential 'country pub' is another unmistakable feature.

Harry Townley

Parsley Hay

Parsley Hay. 25 October 1961: LNWR G2A 0-8-0 No **49391** stands on the back road or "High Peak" road in Parsley Hay Sidings. The reason for this particular road being referred to as the "High Peak" was that it was, prior to the alteration of the layout when the Ashbourne line opened, the High Peak main line, giving direct access to the small sidings or "wharf" which that company provided. It was very awkward for Ashbourne bound freights to place wagons in this siding and "fly shunting" was the method used. This involved setting back down this siding road, coupled to the vehicle to be shunted. The shunter with shunting pole poised between the tender and wagon would signal to the crew to move forward, he running as fast as he could alongside waiting for the driver to make a slight brake application so that the coupling would slacken and so allow him (the shunter) to uncouple the wagon. The locomotive would then accelerate away as fast as possible so that the points leading into the yard could be set so that the wagon could (hopefully) roll into the siding whilst the engine continued up the line. The points would be reset, the loco would set back clear of the points which would be set again for the siding and the engine could proceed into the siding to position the wagon properly. What could go wrong?? (1) The engine might not get out of the way quickly enough. (2) The wagon might stop on the points, that would mean another 'illegal operation' known as "planking" to get the wagon which was half out of the siding back to its starting point again. (3) If the boiler was too full of water (on a Super D) the moment of acceleration away from the wagon would produce a startling display of 'hydraulics' and Parsley Hay signal box might be passed at some speed, so the signal controlling the exit from the sidings needed to be cleared before operations commenced. *J.M.Bentley*

Parsley Hay. 29 March 1965: 4F 0-6-0 No **44587** rostered to work the 1.40 pm Buxton - Briggs, finds itself at Parsley Hay to assist 2MT 2-6-0 No **46401** which is overloaded for the 1 in 60 of Hurdlow bank, with the return Friden - Buxton freight, on this occasion heavily loaded with ballast from Intake Quarry. Driver Bert Smart is seen in charge of the 4F. *J.M.Bentley*

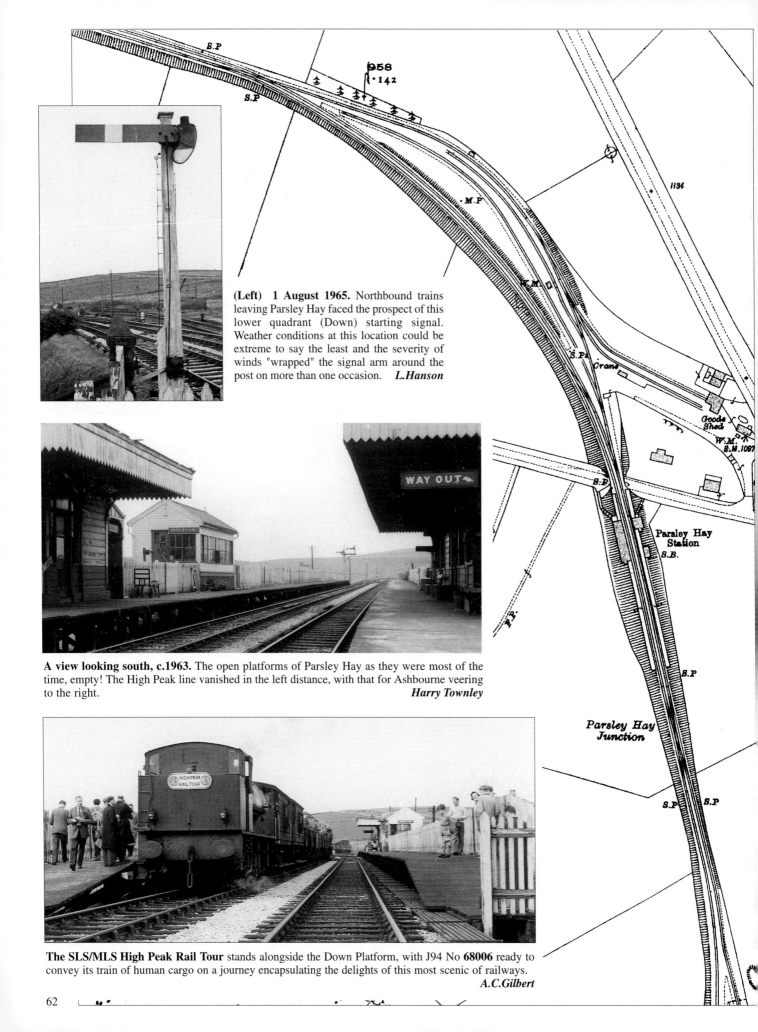

(Left) 1 August 1965. Northbound trains leaving Parsley Hay faced the prospect of this lower quadrant (Down) starting signal. Weather conditions at this location could be extreme to say the least and the severity of winds "wrapped" the signal arm around the post on more than one occasion. *L.Hanson*

A view looking south, c.1963. The open platforms of Parsley Hay as they were most of the time, empty! The High Peak line vanished in the left distance, with that for Ashbourne veering to the right.

Harry Townley

The SLS/MLS High Peak Rail Tour stands alongside the Down Platform, with J94 No **68006** ready to convey its train of human cargo on a journey encapsulating the delights of this most scenic of railways.

A.C.Gilbert

Parsley Hay. Saturday 22 April 1961: 'Fowler' 2-6-4T No **42371** with the ECS of the joint Stephenson Locomotive Society (NW Area) and Manchester Locomotive Society train on the occasion of their tour of the open sections of the C&HPR and certain adjacent lines. Participants made their own way to Matlock for about 11.40 am to join special buses to Cromford Wharf. They then travelled in trains of freight stock to High Peak Junction and back, from Sheep Pasture Top to Middleton Bottom and from Middleton Top to Friden via the Gotham Curve. From Friden the tour continued in passenger stock (above) to Parsley Hay, Hindlow and Old Harpur, then the terminus of the line. After returning to Hindlow the train avoided the Buxton stations via the junctions and proceeded via Peak Forest to Edale, there was a further reversal at Chinley and the tour was booked to terminate at 8pm.   *A.C.Gilbert*

Parsley Hay. October 1961: Buxton G2 0-8-0 No **49406** awaits departure to Hartington with the 9.50am Buxton - Uttoxeter freight.   *J.M.Bentley*

THE ROUTE CONTINUED

HURDLOW TO PARSLEY HAY

Parsley Hay, 18·5 miles was reached at 9.55am. There is a reference in the book 'All about Derbyshire' *to a bridge carrying a road that seems to lead nowhere!* which Dr Hollick identifies as having become the modern A515 Ashbourne to Buxton Road, and a description of Parsley Hay station as, resembling 'something on an American prairie line'. Near Parsley Hay is Newhaven Tunnel (51 yards) under the Ashbourne - Buxton main road. The south face bears the legend "Cromford & High Peak Railway 1825" surrounding a crude wagon, while in the four corners are the letters "P H & Co" presumably the initials of the contractor. The north face shows the crest of the C&HPR - a four-wheeled wagon on a shield, with the motto *Divina Palladis Arte* the whole surrounded by a garter reading **Cromford & High Peak Railway Company. Incorporated 1825**. Above is inscribed **Jos. Jessop, Esq. Engineer** and below **Wm. Brittlebank Esq.** (Brittlebank and Son of Wirksworth were Clerks to the Company). At the south end of Parsley Hay Station the line from Ashbourne curved alongside and the two were connected by a scissors crossing which led into the double line which continued until 1959 from here to Buxton. From PARSLEY HAY, now a focal point with a Visitor Information Centre and facilities on the Tissington Trail which follows the tracks of the former High Peak line, the route continued to Friden, 21 miles where **'The Fly'** was booked to arrive at 10.10am.

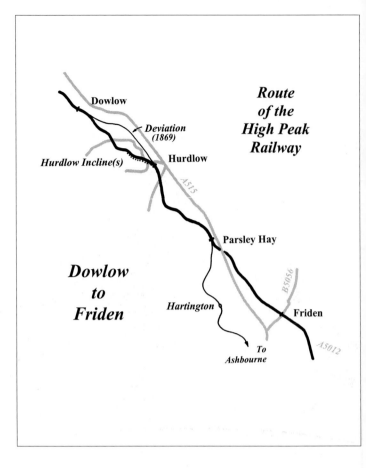

Route of the High Peak Railway

Dowlow
Deviation (1869)
Hurdlow Incline(s)
Hurdlow
A515
Parsley Hay
B5056
Dowlow to Friden
Hartington
Friden
To Ashbourne
A5012

Parsley Hay c.1968. Final obsequies: Future events were foreshadowed when passenger services between Buxton-Parsley Hay-Ashbourne were withdrawn on 1 November 1954. The Middleton Incline was closed 3 June 1963 but the last vestiges of the 'real, old' High Peak line were abandoned in 1967 but that most distinctive feature, the water traffic lasted to the end, and the last places to require rail by water were the railway houses at Parsley Hay and Hartington; although all other traffic, ceased 2 January 1967 the tanks ran until 5 September 1967. When Gregory Fox visited Parsley Hay the sad remains of this former 'legendary' site were the remnants of the signal box and its accoutrements and Water Tank No.19 languishing on an abandoned length of track. In the 'good old days' Cromford Wharf supplied 100 tanks of water per month to various sites along the C&HPR. These 'tankers' were specially built on old tender frames or were old tenders suitably adapted; there was at first, a series of tanks numbered 1 to 19 but this separate listing was abandoned by the LMS and later tanks all of which were adapted tenders were known by the LNWR or LMSR tender number plates which they carried. Nos 18 and 19 in this series were former Webb six-wheeled tenders reduced to four wheelers by the removal of the centre pair of wheels, they had neither tender nor work plates and were identified by the number painted on their sides as on No19 (top right). However, No 19 did not have coal rails fitted and the tank was probably not the original one but a replacement; when the work of conversion was carried out old tenders were fitted with a leading buffer beam - complete with buffers - and a hand-rail for the shunters (Bottom right) Dr. J. R. Hollick records in his notes that a batch of 'water tenders' which included No19 were broken up at Buxton in March of 1968. G.K.Fox

Parsley Hay. 26 October 1961: LNWR G2A 0-8-0 No **49277,** having shunted and weighed the traffic the Friden goods had brought some time earlier, now prepares to run round its train prior to departing for Briggs Sidings and Buxton. The locomotive was working the two day diagram commencing with the previous day's 09.50am Buxton to Uttoxeter freight. The reason for the loco (always a Super D) having to carry out this duty at Parsley Hay was because of shortage of water capacity on the Midland 3F 0-6-0 which had worked this Buxton - Friden turn; working all day on one tank of water by the time Parsley Hay was reached on the return journey just enough water was left to get the engine to Buxton depot.

J.M.Bentley

Parsley Hay. 25 September 1955: Buxton based 3F 0-6-0 No **43268** heads the Ian Allan High Peak Rail Tour W560 through the scissors crossing into Parsley Hay Station. This particular tour ended, for a while, the spate of High Peak special trains, much to the interest of the solitary cow knowledgeably watching events and the photographers, from her stance beside the 1/4 mile post on the left of the picture.

Harry Townley

Parsley Hay. c.1930: The old Roman road, now the A515 highway from Buxton, is just visible on the hillside above the station. The stoutly built, well maintained dry-stone walls mark the divergence of the Ashbourne and High Peak lines; the small underbridge was No.1 on the new line to Ashbourne.

Dr.J.R.Hollick

Northern portal Newhaven Tunnel. 1 September 1964: Above the portal is a stone plaque bearing in raised letters the name of engineer Josias Jessop, and beneath it the Company Crest including a representation of a 'chaldron' type wagon. At the far end of the tunnel Driver Eric Rickman waits patiently with No **46401** as his fireman gets on with his photography; was there ever a line quite like this one? The roundel in the spandrel at the south end portayed a wagon quite different in design.

J.M.Bentley

Brundcliffe Plantation: In this view of the 'HIGH PEAK RAIL TOUR' W574, the train is passing through the Brundcliffe Plantation, travelling away from Friden on its journey towards Parsley Hay and Hurdlow. The 3F's put in years of hard work on this section, they being the largest loco-motives permitted to use the line. When traffic was at its height before the decline in the late 1950's these engines would be expected to shift up to 60 wagons to Parsley Hay, where with an almost empty water tank they would hand over their load to the ex LNWR 0-8-0 on the Uttoxeter - Buxton freight to deal with. The 3F would have done the entire day's work on one tank of water, the area of the High Peak line being to all practical intents water-less, was unable to make any supply available for locomotive needs.

Harry Townley

...between
Parsley Hay
and
Friden

Site of Blakemoor Sidings c.1930's:
When Dr Jack Hollick took this picture on one of his 'expeditions' around the High Peak railway in the 'thirties' the siding had already been removed, but this loading site was typical of many which the building of the railway had attracted; comprising merely a one line siding, a loading platform, with the stone won from a nearby quarry site handled manually and very little else. This siding was No 564 in the London & North Western Railway's "List of Private Sidings" Register.

Dr.J.R.Hollick

FRIDEN

Dr Hollick says when writing of Friden that its original designation of a 'Wharfe', as in canal parlance, was probably more correct than 'Station', as at first it was no more than a siding off the main line supplemented by a small wooden Goods Shed. Friden gained in importance when Mr John West learnt of deposits of clay and ganister sand in the area suitable for making refractory bricks, (high temperature resistant products used in Gas Works retorts), although at first only ordinary bricks were made and fireclay supplied until the end of 1894. To obtain the raw materials to manufacture and market these products, Mr West took out a lease on about 4¾ acres of land, which included farms and pits, and erected his brickworks, the Derbyshire Silica Fire Brick Co., (which became a Limited Company in 1898) beside the existing railway sidings and station of the High Peak Railway, which ran through his new property. The works comprised four bays of sheds with very low roofs, and the plant consisted of a grinding pan driven by an old locomotive engine powered by steam from a vertical boiler, together with a small drying floor. The bricks were made by hand and fired in open-clamp kilns until 1895 when the first beehive clamp was built to replace the clamp kilns. The Friden Pit on company land supplied the demand for raw materials except for a small amount of clay from other parts of the property for the first fourteen years, until the Blakemore Pit was opened in 1906.

Narrow gauge tramlines were laid from the pit to the Works and the sand conveyed in one cubic yard capacity side-tipping wagons in 'trains' of 2 wagons drawn by one horse until Simplex locomotives as built by the Motor Rail & Tramcar Co., of Bedford were purchased to replace the animals in 1923. The DSFB Co, never possessed any narrow gauge steam locomotives.

The old C&HPR railway station being included in the lease was taken over by Mr West but sub-let to the Railway Company for £45 until 1895 when the L&NWR, with whom the C&HPR of course was amalgamated, built a new Friden railway station on the other side of Youlgreave Road. From 1892 to 1894 the station master lived in the Station House and paid rent to the company.

In 1898 the six 'Friden Cottages' to house company employees were built beside the Youlgreave road by JF&C Atkins.

Brick making requires water and until 1897, whilst the first reservoir was being built, water for manufacturing purposes was conveyed to the brick works over the High Peak line in the 'famous' railway tender tanks. When the excavation was formed and 'puddled' to prevent leaks, water was pumped from the Friden Pit to fill this, the first works reservoir. In 1899 pipes were laid from the Black Clay Pit on Oldham's Farm and syphoned into a mere at Friden Hollow and then pumped up to the Works. Other pits on Mr West's land were linked to accelerate the supply of water to the works reservoir. During an exceptionally dry spell in 1918 water was carted from Youlgreave to keep the works going; the Local Authority claimed compensation from the company for damages allegedly caused to the highway by this extraordinary road traffic.

During 1919 a borehole was sunk by Mathews & Co.,Ltd., through solid rock to a depth of 465 feet; estimated to give about 1,000 gallons of water per hour this borehole was later deepened to 577 feet. About 1936 mains water was obtained from the Local Authority but used mainly for drinking and washing purposes.

The moorlands of the 'Low' or 'White' Peak, over 1,000 feet above sea level, may appear bleak and inhospitable, yet they have been settled from prehistoric times. There is evidence that a Neolithic community lived in the area and the moors abound in ringbanks, barrows, and important sites such as that at Arbor Low, an ancient Druid Circle dating back to about the same period as "Stonehenge" situated near to Upper Oldham's Farm. The route of a Roman road passes through Oldham's and Upper Oldham's Farms. There were manors here in Saxon times and the name Friden may come from the Norse, Freya, or Frygga, the wife of Odin, father of the Norse gods. Mr West and his colleagues were interested in the local history and official reports speak of relics such as flint instruments used by ancient men being found on company land and unearthed during excavations in and around the pits and quarries. Several old barrows or burial mounds were, indeed still are, situated on the Company's property.

Hartington is mentioned in the 'Domesday' book, and before the 'Dissolution' there was a monastic grange here, nevertheless before the arrival of the Derbyshire Silica Firebrick Brick Co., it was only the presence of Friden Farm that caused the location to be named on the map. It was this farm and existing pit which Mr West acquired by lease from Squire T.W. Bateman in 1892 ; some silica sand from the quarry had already been supplied to Potteries in Stoke.

Contemporary history (and 'old wives' tales) tell of the coaching era, when the named stage-coaches plying between London and York traversed these moorlands; of the landed gentry and their hunting parties and of blizzard conditions when travellers might be snowbound for days at a time.

Since roads from five directions met at Newhaven close to Friden, small wonder that a hostelry should be found there to succour benighted travellers; there was also a great fair, held on seven acres known as "Fairground" annually on the second Tuesday of every September where farmers and traders from miles around brought their cattle and sheep, hunters and hacks; not only livestock was traded, but foodstuffs, garments, even furniture was on sale with journeymen carpenters peddling their services. Merchants established booths whilst pot-houses competed with the established inn although this, now Newhaven House was not so grand until acquired by the 5th Duke of Devonshire at the end of the eighteenth century. It is thought Architect John Carr of York who was then working at Buxton may have advised the Duke on the design of his extensions to the old property. Today it comprises a moderately sized three storey Georgian block sandwiched between two larger mid-Victorian style buildings. Adorned by a handsome portico the building was a fitting venue for meetings of the Manor Court which were held here until 1871. The greater part of Newhaven House is now a Grade II listed building. Another fair held at Newhaven every 30th October was very much a 'Hiring Fair' where farm labourers and domestic workers could offer their services for a fixed period of time.

At this meeting of the ways the turnpike which had pursued its tortuous way up from Buxton began to fall rapidly towards the Dove Valley. A Royal visitor to 'Newhaven' was George IV King of Great Britain and Ireland. As Prince of Wales he had acted as Prince Regent during the attacks of insanity suffered by his father

continued on page 70

Friden. 1 September 1964: Buxton depot's engine No **46401** disappears into the brickworks with a couple of wagons, cheerfully passing the board forbidding locos to "PASS BEYOND THIS POINT". This was a daily occurrence, these locos would go right into the works between the kilns, they could negotiate very severe curves, and as the floor of the works and the rail top were level, any derailment could soon be dealt with. One of the first introductions for a new fireman on this job was to have a brick thrown at him, on catching it only to find that it was made of compressed sawdust and as light as a feather - these bricks were used to plug inspection holes in the side of the kilns. The Ivatt 2MT 2-6-0's arrived at Buxton in 1962 to take over the duties of the last ageing ex Midland 3F 0-6-0's, whose tenure on this job went back to the later 1920's. Stoke depot loaned No **46429** for the trials which proved very successful and in due course two very dilapidated members of the class arrived at Buxton, No **46465**, described as the *"Pride of Mildenhall"* and No **46480** definitely not the *"Pride of York"* from whence it came. Neither of the pair was fit for much work however, the last 3F No **43213** was stored, but when No **46465** had been sent to the works for repair and No **46480** became unfit for work, the weary old 3F had to be resurrected, but at first refused to make steam at all, causing the cancellation for one day of the Friden turn, and finally, with assistance from Buxton so as to save on water consumption, No **43213** staggered through until No **46465** returned. No **46480** was duly shopped and No **46401** one of the original smaller cylinder engines came to Buxton as spare, but actually took on the role of the regular Friden engine when No **46465** took over the Sheffield passenger turn from the Fowler 2-6-4 tanks. On this picture Buxton Guard, John Magore is seen approaching, 'shunting pole in hand'.

J.M.Bentley

George III. George IV succeeded to the throne in 1820; he sojourned at Newhaven in the course of a journey to Scotland and so enjoyed his stay that he awarded the hotel *"a free and perpetual licence"*. This is understood to have only lapsed in the 1970's when the hotel was closed for extensive repairs.

The modern Friden Works of DSF Refractories & Minerals Ltd and the abandoned route of the Cromford & High Peak Railway, is hidden from Newhaven house by a bank of trees, although a greatly altered and short section of the line near Dowlow, (which is a continuation of the former line from Buxton), remains open to serve the ICI kilns there; the limestone to feed the kilns is no longer quarried locally but comes from Tunstead on the Peak Forest line.

For the first seven years after establishing his company, Mr John West looked after the estate's farms himself with the assistance of farm bailiffs, until 1897 when Mr A. H. West took over their management. In 1902 the farms were leased out to individual tenants. Until 1897 the works were managed in succession by Mr Low, Mr Hodgkinson and Mr Hall. Then Mr A. H. West took charge, followed by Mr Beardmore in 1905 and Mr N.A. Lloyd in 1924. In those early days the Manager in addition to looking after the works did all the bookkeeping, and paid the wages in addition of course to supervising the farms.

Two of the Derbyshire Silica Firebrick Co's., earliest employees were William Featherstone and S. Dale. William Featherstone, who started about 1893-4 looked after the horses, did some tramming in the pits and drove the steam wagon to and from Parwich Pit which the company worked from 1913-15. William retired in 1930 and took over a small-holding which he worked until his death in the late 1950's. His son was then still with the Company, engaged on engineering work. Other early employees were T. Sims mostly outside foreman over the pit workers, he joined the company in 1894 and died in 1925. J. W. Brindley started as Timekeeper in 1905 aged about 17 years, he joined the Forces during the 1914 war but returned to the works in 1917 for 2 or 3 years, and left to become landlord of the Bull Inn at Youlgrave, only to return to Friden Works about 1924-25 to take charge of the pits; he died in 1936.

Some of the "Old Hands" recalled that at the outset they used to dig the raw materials from Friden Pit during the Summer and move into the sheds and make up bricks during the late Summer and Winter months.

In these days of 'short term contracts', worries about job security','working from home', and other pressures engendered by a 'service industry' based economy, the loyalty displayed by the Friden workers and the continuity of their employment does make one think those really could have been the "Good Old Days"!!

For instance:

M. Wagstaff started work at Friden, June 1911, served in the Forces during World War I, returned to the Works, had 38 years service at Friden by 1947, and received his Gold Watch in 1951. He lived until March 1956.

J. W. Evans who started at the Works in 1895, received his Gold Watch and Chain for 50 years service and over in 1947, as did T. Dawson who started in 1894, E. Wood who started in 1896 and W. Wragg, who also started in 1896. T. Palfreyman who started in 1904 retired in 1947 and received a Gold Watch that year.

Other recipients of Gold Watches in 1947 were : J. A. Dawson (46 years service), R. Dawson (45 years service), Lewis Birds (44 years service), W. Wragg (43 years service), C. Bosley (42 years service), Joseph Fearn (42 years service), and G. E. Frost (40 years service).

Another 48 workpeople received long service certificates in 1947 for 30 to 38 years service and 32 received certificates for 25 to 29 years service.

The number of staff employed matched the growth of the business :

1892 - about 8 - 12 employees

1895 .... 18 to 20 employees

1904 .... 31 employees

1905 .... 44 employees

1909 .... 45 employees

1914. Over 80, or 50% of employees enlisted and served during the Great War. Three received decorations and 20 "laid down their lives". Women and girls were employed for the first time, some of them working presses formerly operated by husbands or sweethearts.

A memorial constructed of tablets built into the walls of the Works made of materials from the Company's pits and burnt in the Works kilns was unveiled at a service in the works by His Grace the Duke of Devonshire KG on Saturday 22 July 1922.

1920 .... 188 employees

1942 .... 348 employees including Office Staff

A Memorial to employees who served in World War II was crafted to a design chosen from a number submitted by employees.

The citation at the dedication was:

Friday 11th November 1949.

We are here today to unveil the Memorial to the memory of our comrades who fell during the last War, and I think that Armistice Day is indeed a fitting occasion for this ceremony to be carried out. The number of employees in the Company called up for service in the Armed Forces in 1939/45 was 109 men and 4 women, of those 8 lost their lives and the names of those are inscribed on the tablet.

A footnote stated *"Some may wonder why the name of Jim Birds is left out. It is because he left us and joined the Royal Navy before the outbreak of War."* It does seem a shame that 'Jim' should be excluded by such a 'back-handed' acknowledgement!!

Back in 1940, the Friden works, where air-raid precautions had been taken and sand-bags laid as necessary, was selected as a centre for the Local Defence Volunteers (later of course the Home Guard). Led by Mr N. A. Lloyd, their base was in the Works Canteen and the Unit played a vital role not only in safeguarding the works but protecting the important military traffic passing along the High Peak line.

An average of about 45 Italian Prisoners of War housed in Camps near Biggin, were employed at the works during each of the years 1942/3/4/5.

Friden. 25 April 1953: Standing at Friden after discharging its passengers is the former North London Railway 0-6-0T No **58856** carrying slow passenger headcode, in itself a very unusual occurrence on the High Peak line. This locomotive, originally NLR No 16, a 1907 renewal of the old No 16 built in 1889, became LNW 2876 in 1922, LMS 7515 in March 1927, 27515 in April 1935 and finally 58856 in September 1948. Withdrawal came in October 1957 when replaced by a loco of the LNE J94 0-6-0T type. *E.M.Johnson collection*

The works was illuminated only by oil lamps until 1918 when a steam driven DC generator was installed, the steam engine was replaced by an oil engine in 1926 and in 1928 mains electricity was obtained from the Nottinghamshire & Derbyshire Electric Grid.

An interesting offer was made to the Friden Company in 1924 by Messrs. Bottom's of Oakamoor, on the railway (now in part preserved between Oakamoor, Cheddleton and Leek Brook Junction) which was the Churnet Valley line of the North Staffordshire Railway. Bottom's offered their Works and sand deposits to the DSFB Co Ltd for the sum of £7,000 but they decided to continue working deposits nearer to their Friden works.

What could have been a major disaster but for the sterling efforts of the workers and local people occurred when a fire started at the works at about 9.30pm on Tuesday, 28 December 1920 and spread rapidly to engulf the lower sheds, an area of about 3,000 square yards, destroying the bulk of those units. Men came from Youlgreave, the six Friden cottages, Biggin and Hartington, and as there was (at that time) no works fire engine formed a human line from the front reservoir to the blazing sheds and passed buckets of water hand to hand to quench the fire at various points. Meantime other men, who were company employees cut through the roofs between the top and lower sheds and created a fire-break which prevented the fire from spreading to the top sheds.

The fire brigades from Bakewell, Ashbourne (which had a manual engine) and Buxton were summoned, but the Bakewell 'steam' engine, drawn by two of the Urban Council's heavy cart horses (two more horses were taken on to assist up the hills at Alport) was the only one to come in time, meantime however a Mr Arthur Cresswell of the Old Market Hall, Bakewell had 'motored' three fireman the nine miles to Friden; the engine arrived at 12.35 am and with hoses playing in eight minutes assisted in the final stages of putting out the fire. The Buxton Brigade despite their best efforts over tortuous roads arrived too late.

By June 1921 the debris had been cleared and new buildings and more modern machinery installed. The value of the plant alone destroyed in the fire was around £12,000 and although the company was insured the full amount of the cost of replacement was not recoverable because of the upgrading. A small Works Fire Brigade was formed in 1921 and a manual fire engine was purchased for their use, this was replaced with a 'power' fire engine in 1940.

In 1923 new offices, the canteen and laboratory were built and another although less serious fire which was covered by insurance occurred at Blakemore Sidings in July 1926. Over the years a Sports Ground, Cricket Field, indeed quite a wide range of staff amenities and benefits in accordance with the best practice of the time were introduced.

The Derbyshire Silica Firebrick Co., Ltd., was an important member of the Main Research and Commercial Associations of the Clay Industry, and Directors and Officials held important positions in those organisations. Mr Frank West was President of the Refractories Association of Great Britain (RAGB) in 1929, was on the Council of National Federation of Clay Industries in 1932 and President during the War Years 1941-43.

By this time so many intricate and graceful shapes and mouldings were produced by the Derbyshire Silica Firebrick Company. Ltd., that many of them were considered to be more on a par with pottery than bricks. One of the company's larger pits was described as being 100 yards across with the topsoil removed to expose the sides of the pit which were of weathered limestone, with at one end a deep strata of whitish coloured sand, which changed to veins of yellow, purple, red brown and almost black varieties, containing well-worn quartz pebbles.

As already indicated water was scarce in the Low Peak and supplies for domestic and locomotive purposes were conveyed in special railway 'tender tanks' to stations along the C&HPR from both Buxton and Cromford Wharf, the Cromford supply was tapped from a natural spring on the hillside. Harry Jack, and Dr J. R. Hollick jointly wrote a definitive article on this traffic for the April - June 1985 Journal of the Historical Model Railway Society.

The reasons for the sparsity of water are related to the formation of the deposits of clay and ganister sand found in the area. The deposits are thought to have been laid down in pre-glacial times, a pit being the remains of a 'swallow hole' similar to others known in Derbyshire. They may have taken the waters of a long extinct river that flowed when the whole area was considerably higher than it is today. Near the bottom of the 'swallow' there could have been an outlet or outlets to the underground water tables that became silted up, inducing the formation of a great whirlpool of funnelling water in which particles of sand, gravel and rock detritus would be ground to powder. The works' chemists found that the silica sand so suited to the manufacture of their products contained minute, well-rounded grains of quartz which such a phenomenon as a 'swallow' hole might produce.

During 1892 to 1899 the High Peak Railway only ran from Buxton to Parsley Hay, and carried passengers no further than Parsley Hay, the freight only line then continued on its way to Cromford Wharf and High Peak Junction, passing Friden Station and the D. S. F. B. Co., Ltd., works en-route.

High Peak Line - Some Improvements were :

Buxton - Hindlow - new line 27 June 1892
Hindlow - Parsley Hay - realignment and doubling
1st June 1894
Parsley Hay - Ashbourne - new line - 4 August 1899

In the early days the only way in which Mr John West could get to the works by rail from Manchester was to travel to Parsley Hay station and alight there. When the Parsley Hay - Ashbourne line was opened in 1899 he was able to travel on to Hartington, which was rather nearer to Friden. In both instances he was met by horse and trap and stayed for the duration of his visits firstly at the Newhaven Inn, then from about 1894 at the Station House and from 1897 at Friden House, which the company had built adjacent to the works; one room was made into an office and so used until 1923 when the new offices were built.

The first postal address of the Company was the Derbyshire Silica Firebrick Company Ltd., Friden House, High Peak Railway, near Matlock Bath, Derbyshire, but the company was forced to make so many complaints to the Post Office about late delivery of their mail that in August 1903 the address was altered to Hartington, near Buxton.

As early as 1907 the D.S.F.B.Co., Ltd., was trading internationally with deliveries leaving Friden by rail bound to the docks for destinations as diverse as Copenhagen, Japan and South America. By 1932 "Outside Clients" e.g. other than Gas Works the chore business at the outset, included products designed for electricity, iron and steel works, furnace builders, glass and chemical works and many other industries.

The Directors supported the Peak & West Derbyshire Walling Association's first competition "to keep alive this ancient craft in the Peak District" which was held on Friden Farm and rated a mention in the Daily Dispatch of 9 September 1937; there was a similar competition at Hill Farm, Flagg in 1938.

Also in 1937 a party of about 70 members of the Geological Section of the British Association visited the Friden pits and excavations under the leadership of Professor Fearnside.

Following the cessation of hostilities in 1946 the Derbyshire Silica Fire Brick Co., Ltd., like the rest of industry settled back into peacetime production in a changing environment, and was able to celebrate its centenary on 24 September 1992 with a commemorative plaque, and a Gala and Open Day for its 160 employees, their families and pensioners, but then regrettably it was necessary for a Receiver to be appointed on 6 May 1993.

However under new ownership, and trading as DSF Refractories & Minerals Ltd., the Friden works is still an organisation of considerable importance both in the area and in the sphere of manufacture of its specialised products. Moreover its Directors maintain the original company's tradition of industry leadership, and the present day Managing Director, Derek Whelpton, served as President of the RAGB in 1998/99.

There was great excitement locally when, in June 1932, the first passenger train for 80 years disembarked 250 visitors from the Manchester Society of Engineers. The lists of other visitors over the years held in the company's records would fill several pages of an engineering 'Who's Who', although perhaps the most unusual party comprised an Indian Major and 28 Indian Troops who were welcomed to Friden in 1940.

On 14th June 1940 The Manchester District Junior Association of Gas Engineers, President R. J. Bradshaw M.Inst. G.E. visited Friden and, through the good offices of Derek Whelpton, Managing Director of DSF Refractories & Minerals Ltd., we are able to quote from a booklet that was produced by the company for the visitors:

"Towards the end of the nineteenth century the founder of the Company, Mr John West, foresaw that industrial processes using high temperatures would tend to operate at higher and higher levels. He was looking around for raw materials from which refractories capable of withstanding such temperatures could be made when the Derbyshire Pocket Silicas came to his notice.

Derbyshire Silica Firebrick Co.,Ltd. Thought to date from the 1920's and captioned "The Works at Friden, Hartington, Nr. Buxton" this splendid aerial view depicts most vividly the rolling Derbyshire moorland in which the works was set. It was indeed originally agricultural land, although some silica sand had already been dug out from both Friden and adjoining land at Washmere and supplied to potteries in the Stoke-on-Trent area. It was 1892 when Mr West obtained a lease on Friden Farm and most importantly the Pit, from Squire T. W. Bateman. This might have been what we would now term a "green field" site but much foresight, ingenuity and capital were required to build such a works on virgin soil, especially to deal with materials of which little was actually known at that time. Typical problems were water supply, in an area where that necessity was undeniably scarce, sewage disposal, light and heating for the works, all this at a height of 1,100 feet above sea level. As brick-making on this scale was a new trade in the area all the workpeople had to be recruited and trained. It was the late spring of 1892 when the first sods were cut in preparation for building the works, and brick making commenced, but for common bricks only and fireclay at first until the end of April 1894 when the Company commenced to supply Siliceous Firebricks. From the beginning a few sheds and a stationary steam engine were installed alongside the existing railway sidings and station of the High Peak Railway which ran through the property; the bricks were in these pioneering days made by hand and fired in open clamp kilns. Contrast those small beginnings with the impressive industrial scene in this aerial view. In the lower left-hand corner is the Goods Yard of the 'new' Friden station referred to in the text, and towards the centre of the scene the Youlgreave road runs from left to right beneath the High Peak railway, the reservoirs are a prominent feature beside the road, as are the cottages and Friden House. The relationship between the location of the works and railway is quite explicit and there is an excellent view of the sidings where No **46401** is seen shunting in the scene on Page 69.   *Courtesy D.A. Whelpton*

In 1892 he established the firm to work these materials which, since then, have been used extensively in the gas industry, the steel industry and other industries which operate high-temperature furnaces.

PRODUCTS

The three main products manufactured are "Siliceous" and "Semi-Siliceous" containing 82% to 92% silica. "Dome" diatomaceous insulating and "Peakskil" 95% silica materials. There are also supplementary products which include various jointing cements.

At the lower end of the works are to be seen the various processes used in the manufacture of the "Siliceous" products, the main ingredients of which are the Derbyshire Pocket Silicas. The next production unit to be seen is that for the manufacture of "Dome" insulating products from diatomaceous earth which comes from Northern Ireland, thus making the products wholly British. At the far end of the works "Peakskil" silica products are made from ganisters or silica rock.

PITS

The "Siliceous" sands and clay known as "Derbyshire Pocket Silicas" are found within the carboniferous limestone, but their origin still confounds the geologists. These sands and clays are won mostly by mechanical means from a number of pits, all of which are within three or four miles of the works, and are transported to the works either by diesel locos and jubilee wagons running on a narrow gauge railway or by road lorries.

At the working faces sands and clays are classified according to type and quality, and then conveyed to the works where controlled blending and mixing is done.

Ganisters, which occurs in the coal measures, is the main material used for the manufacture of "Peaksil" products, and is won both from open pits and from mines. It occurs in the area east of Matlock, and is transported to the works by motor lorry.

WORKS

The works are situated in the High Peak of Derbyshire, about eleven miles from Buxton and twelve miles from Matlock, and face the Ashbourne - Bakewell road near to Newhaven House, which is one of the old coaching inns.

The works site occupies seven acres out of the total of eight hundred acres which comprise the firm's estate, the remainder consisting of siliceous sand and clay pits and farmlands.

In general the raw materials such as sands, ganisters and other necessary ingredients enter the works at one side, and the finished products leave from the other side.

Equipment used and method of manufacture for each of the various types of refractory products made are separate and distinct from each other. In the making of "Siliceous" products the raw materials are blended and screened, after which they are conveyed to storage bins. From the bins the raw materials go either to the pugs and from there to the presses, for the manufacture of special shapes, or directly to presses for the manufacture of standards of various sizes. Certain special shapes cannot be moulded by machine, and these are hand-moulded.

All the materials are dried on hollow floors which are mostly heated by the waste steam of the prime movers, and after a day or two the bricks are taken to the kilns for "setting" into stacks for burning. "Siliceous" bricks take approximately four days to heat up, which is achieved by utilising heat in the combustion gases from those kilns which are at that time actually being coal fired. Then for about a day and a half coal is fed into the chamber until maximum heat is attained and this is held steady for a specified period. From this point bricks are cooled down for about eleven days. The total schedule occupies approximately sixteen-and-a-half days.

It is important that kilns are heated and cooled to a closely monitored schedule according to the type of material to be fired. The burning process is perhaps the most important through which the brick has to pass, and great care is taken that nothing is left to chance. From the very first, careful control is maintained by the use of automatic temperature recorders, optical pyrometers and Seger cones. All optical readings are recorded. This care ensures a finished produce of as good shape, as nearly true to size and as free from cracks as is humanly possible.

From kilns goods are "drawn" inspected and loaded into one of two extensive railway sidings running along one side and one end of the works, or are loaded into lorries for despatch by road transport. Materials for export are packed in barrels, and those not immediately needed are placed in storage which is well protected from the weather."

The booklet then continues with detailed descriptions of the production methods for diverse ranges of the company's merchandise and concludes : "The manufacture of "Peaksil" materials from ganisters or silica rock, and the making of insulating bricks were commenced after the first World War. "Peaksil" is used extensively in the Gas and Steel Industries. The very high quality "Dome" insulating products also are used in the Gas and Steel industries, as well as in many other Industries wherever heat conservation is of importance. The output of the plant is approximately two hundred thousand equivalent 9" x 4·5" x 3" squares per week, plus the necessary cements required for setting them."

Visit of
The Manchester District Junior Association
of Gas Engineers.

PRESIDENT - R. J. BRADSHAW, M. Inst., Gas E.

JUNE 14th, 1950.

to

THE DERBYSHIRE SILICA FIREBRICK Co., LTD.

Towards the end of the nineteenth century the founder of the Company, Mr. John West, foresaw that industrial processes using high temperatures would tend to operate at higher and higher temperatures. He was looking around for raw materials from which refractories capable of withstanding such temperatures could be made when the Derbyshire Pocket Silicas came to his notice.

In 1892 he established the firm to work these materials which, since then, have been used extensively in the gas industry, the steel industry and other industries which operate high-temperature industrial furnaces.

Products.

The three main products manufactured are "Siliceous" and "Semi-Siliceous" containing 82% to 92% silica, "Dome" diatomaceous insulating and "Peaksil" 95% silica materials. There are also supplementary products which include various jointing cements.

At the lower end of the works are to be seen the various processes used in the manufacture of "Siliceous" products, the main ingredients of which are the Derbyshire Pocket Silicas. The next production unit to be seen is that for the manufacture of "Dome" insulating products from diatomaceous earth which comes from Northern Ireland, thus making the products wholly British. At the far end of the works "Peaksil" silica products are made from ganister or silica rock.

Derbyshire Silica Firebrick Co. Ltd., Friden. A reproduction from the official "HISTORY OF THE FRIDEN WORKS" of a photograph of the front of the works, taken about 1921 before the Offices and Canteen were built. Points of interest are the wooden bodied 'Butterley' rail wagon left. Four stately cars, one phaeton bodied and a racy sports car occupy pride of place, a farm cart rests in the field and - a motor-cycle combination and light car are parked extreme right? *courtesy D.A. Whelpton*

Aerial view. Derbyshire Silica Firebrick Co., Ltd., Friden Works: The old Friden Station, included in the estate lease, was sublet to the C&HPR until 1895 when the new station was built on the other side of Youlgrave Road.(The spelling Youlgreave was also used). *courtesy D.A. Whelpton*

Friden. Saturday 18 June 1932: This Special Train drawn by a Midland 0-6-0 carrying express passenger headlamps and the Reporting No 78 was run on the occasion of a visit to the Derbyshire Silica Firebrick Co.,Ltd., works by a party of 250 persons (half of whom were ladies) organised by the Manchester Engineering Council, representing many Engineering Companies in the Manchester area; Mr Frederick West of the Derbyshire Silica Firebrick Co., Ltd., was the president of the Engineering Council from 1931 to 1938. It was stated at the time that this was the first and only time that a complete passenger train had travelled over the section of the line from Parsley Hay to Friden Station.

courtesy D.A.Whelpton

Friden. Saturday 18 June 1932: This was a great day for the company and its employees! Special arrangements were made to facilitate the unloading of the visitors at Friden; as there were no platforms, sets of steps were built in the works as seen placed against coach No.15913 and further pairs are noted in use further down the train, opposite to the loading gauge. Open five and ten plank wagons stand in the siding and instructions for internal shunting are chalked on the end of the further wagon. There were also some young people amongst the visitors, the boy in the 'fashionable' flat cap is very interested in the photographer, and several ladies sport the 'cloche' hat of the early 30's. **J.M.Bentley collection**

Friden. Saturday 18 June 1932: Staff members were prominent amongst those welcoming their guests when the train arrived at 3.30pm and local women who undertook various jobs around the plant were on hand, dressed in their newly washed and starched 'pinnies'. Their group carrying with them a very large and handsome Union Flag they formed up in front of the Youlgrave Band who were present to lead the party whom we see crossing one of the narrow gauge railway tracks which led from the pits to the factories.

courtesy D.A.Whelpton

Friden. Saturday 18 June 1932: Taking up a position behind the ladies with the Union Flag, the Eb Euphoniums leading in the front row the Youlegrave Band, doubtless playing a stirring Sousa march lead the visitors and attendant dignitaries into the works.   *J.M.Bentley*

Except for a small amount of clay from other parts of the property, the Friden Pit supplied all the raw materials needed for the first 14 years, until the Blakemoor pit was opened in 1906. Tramlines were laid from the pit to the works and the sand conveyed in one cubic yard capacity horse-drawn tipping wagons, one horse pulling two wagons at a time. During 1923 these small Simplex locomotives were purchased to replace the horse traction and pull longer wagon trains.   *courtesy D.A.Whelpton*

AN ERA ENDS

Ever popular in its closing years, the Cromford & High Peak railway played host to the members of several respected Railway Societies. Some excursions were routed from Buxton to Middleton Top, via Parsley Hay, but the focus of popular interest was directed to the Middleton and Sheep Pasture inclines, and the infrastructure at Cromford Wharf, particularly since the Ladmanlow to Shallcross section had been abandoned for so long. Traditionally, as confirmed by the November 1877 timetable, the "UP" Direction of Travel was officially designated as being from Whaley Bridge to High Peak Junction, but, as through traffic over the line declined following nationalisation, the Working Timetable in the later phases only listed workings, and timings, as between Middleton Top and Parsley Hay, and the direction of travel was reversed so that trains working forward to Parsley Hay from Middleton, were described as Up trains, not Down as formerly; furthermore, trains only worked between Middleton and Hopton, Middleton and Friden (which was used as an interchange station) and Friden and Parsley Hay, excepting for one 'through' train that was a Saturdays only working.

Friden. In 1892 when Mr West, realising the importance of High Class Refractory Materials in Gas Retort Settings, started the brickworks at Friden the High Peak Railway from Buxton only carried passengers to Parsley Hay. As already mentioned the railway station was included in the lease of the estate and sublet to the Railway for £45 until a new railway station was built on the other side of Youlegrave Road. The station master lived in the Station House from 1892 to 1894 and paid rent to the company.   *courtesy D.A.Whelpton*

Products being carefully packed in Railway Pallets, post war. During 1903-5 shipment of Friden goods abroad was a problem because of many breakages in transit, the cure was to reduce the sizes of the packing cases.   *courtesy D.A.Whelpton*

RATIONALISATION - STAFF REDUNDANCIES

In January 1967 the Divisional Manager's Office at Hunt's Bank, Manchester, circulated the précis of a programme, to close the Cromford and High Peak Line, from beyond Friden Goods Yard to its -then- end, at Middleton Top, the closure would include all the private sidings en-route. By this means, and dealing with the remaining traffic "as Buxton" or at depots as the traders preferred, it was anticipated that substantial savings would accrue in maintenance and renewal costs generally, further economies would be made by a revision of working practices, and additional savings could follow from a revision of the number of operating staff required.

Middleton Top was already shut to all but Private Siding Traffic when the Goods Yard at Longcliffe was closed on 6th April 1964, nevertheless in the 12 months ended 1st July 1966.

Friden, 1 September 1964. This photograph depicts the scene looking away from Friden yard in a southerly direction. The telegraph poles at this point are on the left hand side, but switch over as the line approaches Newhaven Road Crossing. *J.M.Bentley*

Newhaven Crossing, 1 September 1964. This picture was taken from just about the same spot as that which we see locomotive No **68079** with its train on the rear cover, the keepers house of which can just be seen in the distance to the right of the railway. *J.M.Bentley*

Newhaven Road Crossing, 25 September 1955. Two former NLR 0-6-0 tank engines Nos **58860** and **58850,** head an enthusiasts special train across the Via Gelia road towards Friden. Luckily for all concerned riding in the open wagons across the open expanses of moorland, the weather stayed very pleasant throughout the journey. The lack of road traffic build up at the closed gates is worthy of note, as is the motor-cycle with a pillion passenger and side-car, and the immaculate Ford Mark 1 Consul parked on the grass verge; this was a delightful model with three-speed gear-box and column change.

Harry Townley

Newhaven Road Crossing, 22 September 1965 Ivatt 2MT 2-6-0 No **46401** stands at the Friden side of the crossing gates, very unofficially indeed. The driver, Eric Rickman, always game to help, realised that his fireman would be able to walk much further towards Longcliffe to meet the High Peak loco if he gave him a lift as far as the crossing, which he duly did, then returning to shunt whilst his mate, complete with camera, set off towards Longcliffe to meet Driver Sam Buckley who was always willing to pick up a "mate" and take him back to Friden. Looking back at all these events, heaven only knows what would have happened had we "come off the road". Tender engines were not allowed to proceed beyond Friden and we did not have the train staff; but that was the "High Peak", very much a 'family affair' with its own way of doing things. And now.....
J. M. Bentley

... *onwards to **Cromford, and High Peak Junction.***

CROMFORD & HIGH PEAK

A story in Derbyshire dialect by John Buxton-Hilton, the White House, West Church Street, Kenninghall, Norwich, NR16 2EN.

"They're us't poke a lot 'o fun at owld Cromford an' High Peak, what w'it passengers gerrin' out fer mushrooms, or ladies after a bunch o' two o' bluebells, and when owld Tho's Beresford w'are on't footplate 'e used t' stop all oewr't place, 'e allus re'kned to set 'is traps on'th evenin' run and then luk at em on't mornin' round. They we'are places w'ar slope w'are that steep they us't to 'ave a stationr'y engine t' pull't trucks an' carriages up. Then't engine went back an' they'd be c'upled t' another at top end, it weer s'posed to be theer, but it seldom weer. It we'ar no'wt for a crawd o' passengers to 'ave to wait for five or five an' ha'fe 'owrs, especially if o'wd Thos Beresford we'ar on, an' the wind lashin' down on 'em from oe'rt Cat an' Fiddle, that 'ad the'er cloath's flapping round 'em like sails ov a China clipper.

Min'd you i t weer not all'us ow'd Thos' fault. They we're times w'en 'ed let watter got off't boil awr som'at like that an w'ot wi' grit in 'is cylinder cocks, an' 'is pistons siezin' up, it we'are not all'us 'im was t' blame. But 'e we'ar man 'o 'me'ny parts we'are Thos! an' drivin' yon' engin' were on'y wön', 'o 'em. Well th' cu'd tell from't tackle as 'e all'us't keep in 'is cab. Thee'r 'is twelve-bore, an 'is traps, an 'is nets, an' 'is spy glass, an' 'is fourteen foot split cane bottom rod, 'an 'is ferrets, t' say n'owt ov 'is concertina, an an o'wd w'udden coop as 'e 'ad fer 'owt as 'e wanted to t'ek 'ome live.

'E never u'st speak 'o drivin' a train, 'e us't call it 'we'arkin 'is way round't. Well 'o coärse I never knew 'im. bu'r I knew Jack Plant as 'ust t' fire för 'im, 'an' 'e cou'd tell a tale o'r two. Thee'r on' time when it we'are a wunder thi' ever got the'are at all. O'wd Thos 'ad bïn rattled orl mornin' en' thet we'are bec'os main regulator valve 'ad worked loose, aen't steam kept shuttin' itself off. E'd jamm't 'andle oppen wi' 'is tea böttle but then 'e'd gon' an lost ha'f 'is tea in't process, then 'e lost one o' 'is ferrets, then 'e lost Jack Plant, 'as 'e'd sent up to a farm för sum eggs, then 'e ran ow't 'o coal! Min'd you I'm not sayin' tender we'are empty, but tha cèn see 'ow it we'are.

Theer' we'ar two o' three cottages 'e 'ad t' pass, an sometimes a lump o' coal 'ould fall off, just as 'e we'ar outside somebody's yard, an if it didna' fall, owl Thos we'ar not beyond givin' it an 'elpin 'and. E' like't t' keep in wi' folk did Thos! But some o' these cottages 'k'um t' expect it 'an this perticler 'mornin, 'ed chucked that much off at one station or another, for't waitin' room fire, or more likely for't porter's room, that 'ed left hissen short. But while 'e were off, scoutin' round for Jack Plant, 'as 'ad stopped off t' mend somebody a kettle, oo'ever it was as 'ed miss't w'it coal, must 'a b'in up 'on't wagon, and helped hissen. Well - 'e 'ad do a spot 'o' thinkin'. 'E' 'ad enuff t' get 'im up to Edge Moor, but not enuff to tek 'im back to'th't '(H) Opton Incline. So 'e 'ad to figger out who it was 'as 'ad pinched it. Then 'e 'ad t' back train t' go a'n fetch it, then 'e got into a feight about it, then is reversin' gear stuck an 'e 'ad to unscrew th' 'andle t' free it, then 'e fund't fire 'ad dropped, so 'e 'ad to scrape clinker out an' start agen, an' that upset 'im 'cos 'e 'ad to break 'is ferret coop up for't kindlin, then e (h)'adn't enough coal or steam for't injector to work, so 'e 'ad to drop fire agen for fear 'o crackin't boiler, an all this time o' coarse e 'ad a train be'int im. Passengers we'are a bit disgruntled, but they didna kick up, on'th old Cromford & High Peak the'ye got us't t'

livin wi'out miracles. Thos even went wi-out a brace o' pheasant so'at 'e didn't lose any more time. But then, w'en 'e got up to't Bunsall Incline 'e reckoned 'is work sheet gid' im six minutes rest before 'e 'ad to turn round, an' 'e insisted on 'avin' that, while 'e supp't Jack Plant's tea. After that they gi'd 'im a try on another line, they put O'wd Thos on't Ashbourne to Buxton, but 'e didna tak' t' it, it weren't same, the'y we'are t'much clockin' on and clockin' off; 'e us't say there were more foremen in't Buxton Sheds than there were cleaners.

So 'e tu'k t'suppin'! From mid-day arrival t' tea time return journey, 'e we'ar in't Green Man 'i Ashbourne, an' 'e us't t' talk about owld days, about 'ow 'ed onst tekken a light engine out, w'out anybody knowin' and 'ad run owl Nellie Brindley up t' Ladmanlow, "I!" an' stood waitn' for 'er in't holler, wi' a little whisper o' steam blowin' off from 'is check valve - she wer't mid-wife tha knows - it were owd Tommy Ashmore as were born that neet. **"I!"**

An' 'e use't to talk about 'is engines, about 'ow tha' didna drive an engine, tha 'ad to nurse it, same as tha' wud an owd collie on't moors, th'ad t' know when it were'na 'appy, but couldn'a tell thi'. But of coarse he were'na safe on't föötplate; if them Dovedale trippers 'ad knownt state 'e we'are in at throttle, they'd a got out an' walked back over th'owd turnpike; mind you that engine could 'a driven itself, it 'ad to some 'at time, 'e once se'd that 'e nearly forgot to stop at Dowlow 'Alt, but then 'e felt brake 'd go on of it's own accord. *It c'ud 'a bin Jack Plant o' coarse.*

Jack knew 'ow to 'andle 'im! 'E' use't t' lu'k owt for't signals and pick up staff, and keep 'is eye on't watter, an they didna 'ave trouble w'it regulator valve these days, the way Owd Thos we'ar 'oldin on to't 'andle to keep 'issel from fallin' out o't cab there we'ar no danger o' it fallin' shut! Then came day when 'e fell out wi' a level crossin' gate at top end o't (H) 'Artington Cuttin'. It we'ar only across an old farm track, it 'ad never bïn shut 'afore, but Owld Thos didna' see it! 'E didna' even know 'ed 'it it, an Jack Plant darena' say a word for feer 'o upsettin' 'im. That's aggravat'n thing, nobody wu'd 'ave known 'owt about it, they'd never 'ave known but that a farmer 'ad backed 'is 'ay tender or some'at into it, on'y they f'un a piece 'o cross palin hangin' on to Owld Thos' front buffer, when cleaner kem rownd with half a dozen foremen in't mornin'.

THEY GIVE IM'T SACK! An' Owld Thos got a job game keepin' right we'are 'e used to do 'is own rabbitin' on'y 'o coarse 'e cud'nt tek coal round't cottages eny more, only an owld (h)'now and then, 'or a grouse or two in season. They give 'im a nice little chestnut cob to go roun't warrens on, "Owd Newt for Newt" 'e us't' call it, "Get into reverse now Newt for Newt" 'e us't t' shout, "Blast they axle-box". An if 'e wanted a short cut to go down to't Bridge (Whaley Bridge) or up to Long '(H)'ill, 'e used to ride it through thow't owld Burbage Edge Tunnel; horse didna care for that though, it us't t' come out at far end losin' a bit of steam at its blower pipes as Owld Thos us't put it. Ot coarse 'e 'ad more time for things 'e we'are interested in, but 'e allus us't reckon that 'e couldn't do 'is rounds on a pony way 'e 'ad on 'is old engine. **THEY DONN'A RUN RAILWAYS THESE DAYS THE WAY THEY US'T TO!"**